BOLLINGEN SERIES LXXXIII

THE NWARD

TURN OF NARRATIVE

ERICH KAHLER ,1885 -1970

*Translated
from the German by
Richard & Clara
Winston*

*Foreword
by Joseph Frank*

BOLLINGEN SERIES LXXXIII

PRINCETON UNIVERSITY PRESS

THIS IS THE EIGHTY-THIRD IN A SERIES
OF BOOKS SPONSORED BY BOLLINGEN FOUNDATION

Translated from "Die Verinnerung des Erzählens,"
in *Untergang und Übergang* (Munich:
Deutscher Taschenbuch Verlag, 1970)

Library of Congress Catalogue card number 72-4036
ISBN 0-691-09891-3

PRINTED IN THE UNITED STATES OF AMERICA
BY PRINCETON UNIVERSITY PRESS,
PRINCETON, NEW JERSEY

Durch alle Wesen reicht der eine Raum . . .
Weltinnenraum.

—RILKE

Foreword

FEW CONTEMPORARIES could match Erich Kahler (1885-1970) in the immense erudition, the penetrating synoptic vision, and the responsive aesthetic sensibility that he brought to bear on the analysis of the modern world. The present small volume, the first to be published since Kahler's death, is a fine example of his achievement as a literary critic; but it is only a small sample of his life's work, much of it still untranslated into English. For Kahler belongs to the great German tradition of the polyhistor, the tradition whose origins go back to Herder and Hegel, and which has been continued up through the twentieth century by men like Oswald Spengler, Wilhelm Dilthey, Ernst Troeltsch, Max and Alfred Weber, Karl Jaspers, and Ernst Cassirer. Erich Kahler belongs with these great names of the impressive German tradition destroyed by Hitler; and it is only in relation to this tradition that his work can be properly appreciated.

What marks out this line of writers and thinkers is the universality of their ambitions, and their admirable ability to master the intellectual resources necessary to carry these ambitions through. All are inspired by a vision of the *unity* of human history (history seen primarily in terms of cultural forms, whether of science, art, religion, or philosophy—the history, in other words, of an enlarged and modernized version of Hegel's Absolute Spirit), and all undertake to portray the grand sweep of this unity on a majestic scale. Erich Kahler's *Man the Measure*, the major work which he wrote and published in English after his arrival in the United States, is a book which fits squarely into this tradition, and displays a remarkable mastery of the most diverse fields of knowledge as well as the power to mold this vast material into an illuminating and organic conceptual synthesis. Kahler's book, in a certain sense, may indeed be considered a culmination of this tradition. For what he argues, and undertakes to demonstrate, is that the whole course of history itself has been advancing to the *self-consciousness* of the actual and ever-growing social-political unity of mankind which the tradition had previously accepted only as a philosophical postulate.

Another important facet of this German tradition of philosophical history is its acute feeling for the symptoms of cultural crisis. Implicit in its ambition to encompass *all* history, of course, is an awareness of the rise and fall of civilizations and the inevitable flux of historical change. Such an awareness derives from its own origins at the end of the eighteenth century, when all observers could sense the imminent collapse of the Christian-classical civilization that had dominated Europe since the Renaissance. The great works of this school, beginning with Herder's *Ideas on the Philosophy of History of Mankind* and Hegel's *Philosophy of History*, were all attempts to deal with the crisis of culture posed by this collapse, and to offer some basis for its reconstruction and renewal (or at least some intellectual consolation) in the face of the major social and economic transformations that were wiping out the old order for good. This task, needless to say, became more and more pressing and more and more difficult as the nineteenth century wore on; by the twentieth century it had begun to seem almost impossible. But the writings of this school, nonetheless, continued to supply the Western world with the deepest and most powerful diagnoses of its own spiritual maladies.

To verify this assertion, one has only to open the pages of Erich Kahler's *The Tower and the Abyss*—a work which will unquestionably remain as a classic expression and analysis of the situation of modern culture in the years immediately following the Second World War, when the revelation of the Nazi concentration camps and the horror of the holocaust were still fresh in everyone's mind. Like his close friend and admirer, Thomas Mann, whose superb *Doctor Faustus* is the greatest work of art to have emerged from the agony of German (and Western) culture during the Hitler years, so Erich Kahler devoted himself to studying the same phenomena from the point of view of the cultural historian. The result is a book whose disquieting insights earned the praise of such disparate figures as T. S. Eliot and Lewis Mumford, and which, twenty years after its publication, still has more to tell us about modernity than the clamorous vociferations of the new breed of publicity-intellectuals preaching the gospel of salvation through electronic voodoo and multimedia pandemonium.

What has occurred, as Erich Kahler explains, is the steady evolution of consciousness in the direction of the demythification and secularization of wider and wider areas of human life. Since the end of the eighteenth century, this process has been accompanied by the transformation of the human environment through the practical applications of scientific discovery, i.e., technology. Mankind—or at least that part of it living in advanced industrial society—has thus become detached from the ancient certainties provided by religion and cultural tradition; it lives mentally and physically in a universe it has not yet learned how to assimilate emotionally. The spiritual crisis of the modern era is precisely this gap between the mind of the human species and its psyche. In *The Tower and the Abyss*, Kahler chronicles the course of this estrangement, this self-alienation of the modern spirit (these words, now debased to the level of a mindless slogan, have an exact significance in his pages), with broad and graphic strokes, and he finds reflections of this condition in a distressingly wide span of material.

Beginning with the stylistic developments of modern art and literature, Kahler details the gradual loss of contact with the natural world of common-sense experience observable in all of the greatest products of the modern artistic sensibility. Characteristic of this culture, as a result of the impact of the ever-increasing rationalization and mechanization of life, is the exploration of the unconscious, the new awareness of the existential fragility and meaninglessness of existence, and, as a desperate reaction, the frenzy of nihilistic negation which began with Italian futurism and continued in dada and surrealism. (Kahler's book was written before the more recent explosion of pop culture on the international scene, which carries this movement to a paroxysm of cultural masochism and destructive self-hatred; but he has dealt with it in his undeservedly neglected *The Disintegration of Form in the Arts* [1968], a remarkable performance for a man over eighty, and one of the few attempts to grapple with this development in a spirit both comprehensive and severely critical at the same time.) In any case, what makes *The Tower and the Abyss* so revealing and so frightening is that Kahler shows how the same historical factors which can be used to explain the subtlest features of avant-garde art can also be seen at work in the abominable monstrosities of the Nazi concentration-camp world. Both reveal, in different ways, the breakup of the human personality caused by the historical evolution of consciousness—a consciousness severed (ironically enough, by its own achievements) from the unconscious sources of value which, in the past, have always sustained the coherence of the human personality.

Art has always stood at the center of Erich Kahler's world as the most sensitive seismograph of the state of the cultural psyche. This is hardly surprising for a man as closely involved as he himself was with some of the greatest figures in modern German literature. A devoted friend of Rilke's; a member of the Stefan George group, though always harboring reservations about the anti-democratic tendencies of the *Kreis*; an intimate of Thomas Mann's, particularly during their years of common residence in Princeton; the man who shared Hermann Broch's loneliness and solitude in the United States for many years, and in whose home Broch lived (I shall never forget Kahler casually reaching under the couch in his study one day to pull out a dusty typescript copy of *Der Tod des Vergil*, with a dedicatory poem); the cherished correspondent of the most gifted, tragic, and haunted figure of the new generation of German poets, Paul Celan, who wrote to Kahler out of the blue one day after reading one of his articles—these are some of the people who found in him a spirit that could measure up to their own. One should also add that, as a hobby, Kahler made superb translations into German of the modern English poetry (Yeats in particular) that he had grown to love. It is little wonder that Kahler's literary criticism (his essays collected in *Die Verantwortung des Geistes*, his pioneering study of *Die Philosophie Hermann Brochs*, his definitive essay *Stefan George, Grösse und Tragik*) should instantly have been recognized as of permanent importance. The same is true for the splendid series of essays on the history of narrative which have now been rendered into English.

The outstanding merits of this work will be immediately clear to any reader; but he should also know that Kahler's book fills a genuine gap in the critical literature. For despite the importance of the novel as a form in the last two centuries, there are, surprisingly, very few works that attempt to treat the history of the genre as a whole. Special studies abound, to be sure, and some of them, like Ian Watt's *Rise of the Novel*, are of great value. But such works are usually limited to one or another national literature, or, like the noteworthy *The Nature of Narrative* by Robert Scholes and Robert Kellogg, are more concerned with general categories than with history. John Dunlop's *History of Fiction* (1845) is little more than a compendium of plots. Frederick Warren's turn-of-the-century *A History of the Novel Previous to the Seventeenth Century* (a stimulating book that should be rescued from oblivion) is written by an American scholar with a sharp eye for the sociology of literature and who has little to learn from the Marxists; but it is now sadly out of date. There is thus no recent work which surveys the history of narrative up through the end of the eighteenth century in as magisterial a fashion as Kahler's, and which handles all the major problems with a comparable grasp. Only Ortega y Gasset's *Meditations on Don Quixote*, with its brilliant remarks on the relation of the epic to the novel, may perhaps be mentioned as of similar stature; but Ortega makes no pretensions to Kahler's historical sweep.

To be sure, not all of Kahler's emphases and ideas will go uncontested, especially in Anglo-American criticism. The importance he accords to *Gulliver's Travels* and to *Tristram Shandy*, for example, are likely to strike English readers as quite out of kilter. One reason for this discrepancy is that Kahler is writing partly within the context of German literature and with reference to the

German Romantic novel; here the influence of Sterne is much greater than in the English or French nineteenth-century novel. *Gulliver's Travels* appeals to Kahler because he discusses the seventeenth century in terms of the new modes of perception inaugurated by the era of scientific discovery; and Swift not only later produced the greatest narrative work employing these new modes, but also used them to reveal the dehumanizing possibilities of science itself in a prophetic fashion. Swift's relevance to modernity is what gives his book importance for Kahler; the same is also true for Sterne, the precursor of the stream-of-consciousness and the experiments with time so typical of the modern novel.

Indeed, one of the most original features of Kahler's book is that he draws his line of historical continuity, not from the nineteenth-century novel of realism as the presumptive culmination of the form, but from the fractured perspectives and heavily conceptualized creations of the contemporary epic. In this respect, Kahler's work is truly the first *modern* attempt to come to grips with the subject, and to carry out, for the history of the novel, T. S. Eliot's injunction constantly to reorganize the history of the artistic past in terms of the masterworks of the present. This should stimulate, if not a rethinking of the more conventional point of view, then at least a good deal of controversy.

Also, at a time when the cry has gone up in Anglo-American criticism to relate literature once again to the wider horizons of life, the example of Kahler should prove a potent and productive stimulus. For Kahler views the internalization of narrative—the movement from external action and epic adventure to the ever-deeper and more intense exploration of character and personality—as part of the general evolution of human consciousness as a whole. The history of civilization in all its aspects is constantly at his fingertips, and brought to bear at each new twist and turn of the road; but this does not mean that artistic values are discounted, ignored, or deprecated. There is no conflict for Kahler between the closest attention to matters of form and the widest ranging awareness of the historical pressures that condition both formal changes and thematic novelty: and this is as it should be.

I have now said everything I think necessary on this occasion about Kahler the historian and literary critic; but I cannot resist the opportunity to conclude these remarks with a few words about Erich Kahler the man as I came to know him in his later years. For Erich Kahler was a remarkable human being, a person of great kindliness, human warmth, and an overflowing generosity of spirit.

Nothing about him at all, as might perhaps be supposed, suggested a stiff and self-important German *Gelehrter*. On the contrary, the absolute simplicity and spontaneity of his manner and demeanor contrasted oddly, and very appealingly, with what one knew of his formidable culture and his intellectual achievements. There was something endearingly childlike about him, even in, and perhaps particularly because of, the ripeness of his years—an impression which derived from the direct emotional immediacy of his responsiveness, and his unquenchable zest for, and enjoyment of, life. To watch Erich Kahler eat a lobster, as I once did during a memorable lunch at an open-air restaurant on Cape Cod, was both a lesson in the anatomy of crustaceans and a sheer pleasure at participating in a life-giving and life-enhancing ritual. Both the irresistible joie de vivre and the natural capacity to raise this to the level of a dis-

criminating and civilized connoisseurship were typical
of the man and part of his charm.

There is a simplicity of youth, of innocence, and of
naïveté; and, to use a phrase of the French poet Yves
Bonnefoy, there is what can be called *la seconde simpli-
cité*, the simplicity which comes when the bitter lessons
of life have taught one to unlearn all that is merely
factitious, superfluous, and socially imposed. Erich Kahler's simplicity was of this second kind, and what had
remained with him was the pure essence of a soul of the
very mildest and gentlest temper (in the full, original
meaning of the word "gentle," signifying not only sweetness of disposition but also elevation of character). As
Thomas Mann wrote in 1945, on the occasion of Erich
Kahler's sixtieth birthday, his heart was "one of the
warmest, wisest and most willing to give aid."

People streamed in to see him from all over the
world—in such profusion, indeed, that in his later years
his friends would often remonstrate with him at the ex-
hausting expense of time and energy involved. But he
would always reply, with the shy and guilty smile of a
little boy being rebuked for some minor breach of etiquette, and with a helpless shrug of his shoulders, that
his friends were of course right, but still, there might be
something he could do and some way he could help; one
never knew in advance. Just a few days before his death,
when I saw him in the hospital for the last time, he
spoke not of himself but, with his hands clasped before
him as if in prayer, and with a passion that made his
voice tremble and tears come to his eyes, of the terrible
psychic burden—the burden of being both a great German poet and a young Central European Jew growing
up in the shadow of the concentration camps—which
had led to the suicide of Paul Celan.

Erich Kahler's ideal, his hope for the future, was a utopian and communitarian one—not so very far removed, really, from that of the present groping experiments among the youth, but of how different a moral substance! And he loved to dwell on the accomplishments of groups such as the Israeli kibbutzim and various communal experiments in France in restoring a lost equilibrium and harmony to human life even under the most extreme and adverse conditions. "We must . . . establish the human community in our own sphere," he wrote in the first essay in *Untergang und Übergang*, his last volume. "Only if we establish a human community can humanity as a whole be saved." Whether this ideal is more than utopian only the future can tell; but one found it very easy to believe in the presence of Erich Kahler himself. For while he never said one word about any of this in private conversation, the infectious radiance of his personality succeeded in creating around him the sort of community of which he dreamed. He had truly established the human community in his own human sphere; one could believe in it because it existed there, and with him.

Those who were privileged to belong to this community—the community of the friends of Erich Kahler—will always remember him with love, and will never cease to honor and revere his memory.

JOSEPH FRANK

Translators' Note

Die Verinnerung des Erzählens first appeared in *Die Neue Rundschau* 68 (1957) and 70 (1959). It was reprinted in the paperback collection *Untergang und Übergang* (Munich: Deutscher Taschenbuch Verlag, 1970). The present translation has been made from a revised version that Erich Kahler was preparing in the last months of his life. He made a number of minor corrections and additions, eliminated one very long footnote, and rewrote the introductory remarks so that they would form a preface. Had he been able to follow his usual practice, he would have worked closely with the translators on the English version, suggesting alternatives, recommending simplifications, often reconceiving whole passages because his fine attunement to English enabled him to think differently in his adopted language. It is our loss and the reader's that this collaboration is no longer possible.

Several different versions of the Preface were found among Erich Kahler's papers. The translators wish to express their gratitude to Alice Kahler and Theodore Ziolkowski for their help in establishing the author's final intentions.

Unless otherwise indicated in the notes, the English versions of quoted French and German texts are our own.

RICHARD AND CLARA WINSTON

Acknowledgment

Quotations from *The Princess of Cleves*, by Madame de La Fayette, as translated by Walter J. Cobb, are copyright © 1961 by Walter J. Cobb and reprinted by arrangement with the New American Library, Inc., New York, N.Y.

THE INWARD TURN OF NARRATIVE

Preface

My PURPOSE here is to show the vast changes in the modern novel as the consequence of a process that has been at work throughout the whole history of Western man. That process is the transformation of man's reality, of which the transformation in the forms of art is one expression. If we wish to understand what has happened to the novel, we must grasp both the transformation of our reality and the transformation within man's consciousness. Literary history will be considered here as an aspect of the history of consciousness.

Art is more than art, literature more than literature. The arts are forms of expression for human life and experience, and as such they register changes in the condition of man over the ages. But they are also more than forms of expression, and they do more than merely register. By giving expression to latent reality, and thus bringing it to consciousness, they make wholly real what has been only potential. They create the cultural atmosphere of each given age. And by virtue of this function they play as active a part in man's development as other, seemingly more practical human activities such as science, technology, and politics. The evolution of artistic forms of expression is one of the most important evidences we have for the changes in man's consciousness and the changes in the structure of his world. Only when viewed in terms of this dualistic aspect—the development of consciousness and the development of the reality corresponding to it—do the arts gain their full human significance.

The transformation of man's consciousness and the transformation of the reality that this consciousness must deal with combine into a single coherent process. In fact, man himself has developed by means of the perpetual interaction between consciousness and reality, between his interior world and his exterior world. As a result of the growth of consciousness, man's outer world expands and changes. The reality in which man moves and which he must manipulate changes in extent and character. And his experiencing a changed reality in turn propels consciousness onward. The world we experience today is a dynamic one, and we can no longer close our minds to the idea that man, the human race, has a life-span and undergoes the changes of age even as an individual does. Early, mature, and highly civilized man are not the same man; their consciousness is not the same. And similarly, the reality of classical antiquity, of the Middle Ages, of the Renaissance, of the eighteenth, nineteenth, and twentieth centuries is not the same reality.

The dramatic event we call "the arts" takes place in the arena of this interaction between consciousness and reality. The arts, moreover, are far more intensively and directly involved in this interaction than science, technology, or economics. The various spheres of human action are related in multifarious ways; for they are after all differing expressions of one and the same life. Naturally they exert mutual influence upon one another. But even more significant is the fact that these differing human activities display the most astonishing parallels in their peculiar, formally independent and specifically technical developments. The arts, for example, in pursuing their own particular courses have arrived at the same disintegration and transcendental obliteration of the objective world of the senses as has physics—and at the very same time. The same evolution of consciousness and of the reality corresponding to that consciousness can be demonstrated in the most variegated kinds of human expression—and consequently in the transformation of art forms as well. Here I intend to demonstrate it by changes in the forms of narrative.

Every development moves in a definite direction. The direction of the interacting development of consciousness and reality is shown in the following pages to be a progressive internalization of events, an increasing displacement of outer space by what Rilke has called inner space, a stretching of consciousness. This in turn brings with it an incorporation, an internalization, of more and more of the objective world—which means taking in a wider range of the world, and plumbing it more deeply. In penetrating into unexplored strata of reality, consciousness transforms that reality. Thus consciousness changes its world and changes itself. In a much higher and more complex sense the process resembles what happens in a child who tries to master wider and wider circles of his external world. By his efforts to organize that world he becomes aware of his own inner world as a coherent self. By objectification of the outer world he takes possession of his inner world. And in the course of distinguishing and detaching the self, the great confrontation begins between the inner and the outer world, between consciousness and reality. The inner world opens up in a twofold manner—in feeling, ever richer sensibility, and also in rational, intellectual grasp. Thus the inner world becomes increasingly packed with material from the outer world, and in its turn exerts a transforming effect upon the outer world it has acquired.

The great dual process of internalization of reality takes place analogously in the human species. Realms of the external world which were previously obscure, with which man communicated naïvely and unconsciously, with which he was entangled in the confused depths of his being, are gradually subjected to observation and analysis. That is, they are separated and made objective, converted into objects. Not only the external realms but also man's internal realms are thus objectified. But to objectify means to make conscious. So consciousness arises. And by making more and more of the outer world conscious, man constantly draws outer space into his inner space, into an inner space newly created by consciousness. The world is integrated into the ego, into the illuminated self. Thus the dual process paradoxically leads to an ever-intensified objectification of both the outer and the inner worlds, and hence ultimately to an ever greater subjectification of the world. As man objectifies himself he takes the world more and more into himself, which is equivalent to the denaturing of nature. Some of the examples that follow will make my meaning clearer.[1]

For numerous reasons, personal as well as objective, our analysis stops at the end of the eighteenth century,

[1] It will remain for part II of this study to show how the process of internalization has worked out individually and formally; that is, how the selectivity of consciousness in individual narrators has qualitatively changed the reality of each given era. Reality as painted by the narrators of different ages looks different, of course. But in addition, the realities of contemporaneous writers differ according to their social and individual predispositions. We must learn to view reality as entirely dynamic. Erich Auerbach's fine and important book *Mimesis* (trans. Willard R. Trask [Princeton, 1953]) makes a fundamental error in assuming that reality is a stable thing, always the same for all ages and persons, and that different writers have merely approached it in different ways. In fact, the reality of any given period is the product of struggling and advancing consciousness. It seems to me that there is a growing comprehension of this dynamic picture of reality. This is expressed in a remarkable book by Richard Brinkmann, *Wirklichkeit und Illusion* (Tübingen, 1957).

where one stage of development reaches its end and all the elements of narrative culminate in a decisive work, *Tristram Shandy*. This book, which might be compared to a knowingly and artfully arranged bouquet of wild-flowers, anticipates the modern novel, all of whose devices and strategies may be found within it. In the nineteenth and twentieth centuries the novel has become the leading literary form. This period has produced many masterpieces, works of enormous diversity, reflecting as they do the national, social, and stylistic problems of their time and place, as well as the interconnections among these problems. But the basic structures of nineteenth- and twentieth-century fiction had their foundations in previous centuries. Romanticism, realism, naturalism, symbolism, and psychoanalysis with its techniques of inner monologue, stream of consciousness, and free association are only the latter-day versions of subtle and complex procedures present in earlier literatures. Moreover, these various modern trends have already been sufficiently analyzed by many excellent critics, so that we need not touch upon them here. Hence we will remain within the limits we have set for ourselves and focus our attention on the basic elements of narrative as they emerge in the great classic works of the past.

INITIALLY, the process of internalization of narrative consists in gradually bringing the narrated material down to earth and breathing into it a human soul. Narrative begins with cosmogonies and theogonies. Slowly, then, the themes descend to the level of annals and chronicles, to the recording of specific earthly events. Gods are incarnations of native and foreign tribal powers. Mythologies are the personifications of tribal struggles for existence and of group anxieties, projected into a still-unconquered external world. Modern researches have found the source of myths in rituals; but rituals are simply magical modes of intercourse with as yet uncontrolled elemental forces. The early epics— Homer and the Eddas, to keep within our Occidental sphere—document the transition from the mythic to the heroic human realm; but the hero too continues to represent his region and tribe. We know today that these great epics condensed around historical events and migrations, that they represent complex elaborations and reshapings of real happenings. We know that Troy existed and was destroyed several times; we know about Mycenae and the wanderings of the Greek tribes; and we theorize that the princes of the *Iliad* were probably projections back into the past of tribal rulers of the Homeric period. Similarly, the Eddas are a mingling of mythic elements with historical incidents of the Burgundian and Hunnic invasions. The Biblical stories are historical records to an even greater extent. So it is important to note that all these early epics are not mere fictions in our sense of the word, that is to say, not pure inventions. Rather, along with their ancient mythic materials they reproduce, at the core, real happenings, or at the least *believed* realities.

In these first great epic works, especially in Homer and the Bible, we already find man's spiritual nature fully exposed. That in itself signifies a very early internalization of raw event. By stirring the imagination narration itself—in contradistinction to mere chronicle—provokes feeling. If we compare the oldest epic work we know, the *Gilgamesh*, with the *Iliad* and the Old Testament, we observe that in it man is increasingly brought down to earth, is liberated from his primal link with the elemental powers. Even in this epic of remotest antiquity there is a breakthrough to expression of man's inner life. We find in the *Gilgamesh* the first stirrings of human personality; the human element is there even in the depiction of the gods.

All three of these great epic documents contain moving accounts of friendships: Gilgamesh with Enkidu, Achilles with Patroclus, David with Jonathan. The setting of the Babylonian epic is still entirely within the primal mythic chaos; what is specifically human has not yet been vouchsafed a sphere of its own. Gods, demons, and human beings partake of one another's characters, alternate with one another. Gilgamesh is two-thirds divine and only one-third human. Enkidu, his extreme opposite, is still less human. Rather, he is a hairy animal demon, at home in the fields and the mountains, constantly "with the game,"[1] which he protects from hunters. "His whole body is [cov]ered with hair, the hair of (his) head is like (that of) a woman; / The locks of the hair of his head sprout like grain. . . . With the gazelles he eats grass; / With the game he presses on to the drink-

---

[1] Alexander Heidel, *The Gilgamesh Epic and Old Testament Parallels*, 2nd edn. (Chicago, 1949), p. 20, l. 6.

ing-place; / With the animals his heart delights at the water."[2] After the two-thirds god overcomes the animal-man in a duel, a close friendship springs up between them.

This friendship, the human core of the story, delves into the genesis of the human spirit. It is as if both the divine and the human side were striving to become man, and this impulse to attain humanity seems to be expressed in friendship. The animal-man "seeks a friend" with whom he can communicate.[3] The god-man has been a lonely despot, a scourge to his people. Friendship diverts and appeases him, and his friend's death makes him aware of his own mortality.[4] In Gilgamesh's lament for the dead Enkidu, human feelings have already found expression in language.

Achilles, it is true, is a demigod, and the decisive action of the *Iliad* takes place among the gods, whose intrigues are constantly obstructing the aims and acts of men. The influence of the gods even affects single strokes in individual battles. But the different spheres are already clearly distinguished. The gods in their realm are just as humanized as the men. Even if we allow for the fragmentary nature of the *Gilgamesh* text as we have it, there can be no doubt that the articulation of human experience in the Homeric epic is far beyond that of the Babylonian epic, whose expressiveness is still very limited.

In the Old Testament, finally, complete humanness is revealed. Man is wholly man, nothing but man, and he is free; his freedom is founded upon God's covenant with him. Whatever he does is entirely his own doing, for from the very beginning he has been confronted with a choice. In the *Iliad* variegated conversations among men

[2] Heidel, p. 19, ll. 36-37, 39-41.
[3] Heidel, p. 22, l. 41.   [4] Heidel, pp. 78-79, ll. 21-22.

and gods give vivid life to the whole work. These colloquies are far more lively and eloquent than the clumsy dialogues in the *Gilgamesh*. In the Bible, however, all the discourse among individuals is overwhelmed by the one great dialogue between man and God. David, in contrast to Achilles and Gilgamesh, is utterly a sinful human being, entangled in his purely human conflicts. And because of this very preponderance of the earthly element, his lament for Jonathan becomes far more moving than Gilgamesh's lament for Enkidu, though it strikes a similar note, or even than Achilles' keening for Patroclus.

But we must point out an additional nuance. Neither in the *Gilgamesh* nor in the *Iliad* are the relationships between friends presented as being on the same plane as relationships with women. The former are spiritual, the latter, no matter how passionate, merely physical. It is true that the Homeric goddesses are powerful beings whose intervention can be decisive, and there are hints of deeper relationships between mother and son as well as between spouses: Thetis and Achilles, Hector and Andromache, and—in the *Odyssey*—Odysseus and Penelope. But even in this last case, the moving scene of reunion chiefly deals with whether the marriage bed has remained untainted. In this early phase of Hellenism, at any rate, the fundamental difference between men's relationships to friends and to women is accepted as totally natural and therefore does not even rise to consciousness. In David's lament for Jonathan, on the other hand, there is a passage which by its very stress on the nature of friendship brings woman into the question and therefore testifies to a new awareness of man's relation to woman: "Thy love to me was wonderful, passing the love of women."[5]

[5] II Samuel 1:26.

Along with such distinctions, the growth of sensibility and of poignance in expression can be observed in a wealth of episodes both in Homer and in the Bible. I need only recall old Priam's plea for the body of his son, the encounter with Nausicaa, Odysseus' homecoming, the scene among the Phaeacians in which Odysseus, unrecognized, hears the bard sing of his dispute with Achilles and cannot keep back his tears; or the pithy evocation of Saul's state of mind when he visits the witch of Endor; or the story of Uriah in all its complexity: the evidence of Uriah's loyalty to his fellow soldiers, so strong that he refuses to sleep in his house while they must sleep in the open. What a contrast this is with the abominable duplicity of the king! And then comes the message of Joab, the commander, which in a single short sentence confirms his own obedience and the dire consequences of his carrying out the king's instruction: "And your servant Uriah the Hittite is dead also."[6] In this message, wherein he reports the high death toll of an action that ran counter to military logic, he stands fully before us in all his spare, hard, soldierly gravity. He is a personality like Hagen in the *Nibelungenlied*, strong-willed, pitiless, and even cunning, but unshakable in his devotion to the king. In all such passages, the human spirit of those early times comes very close to us.

We can see a further advance in Virgil's *Aeneid*, the first rounded-out, deliberately composed epic; in addition to its echoes of Homer it displays strict artistic organization. In the *Aeneid* we have a poem that already rests fully and firmly on the solid earth. Here the origins of Rome are being transformed into myth—in retrospect, from the viewpoint of the Augustan Empire and with the political aim of furnishing that empire with a histori-

[6] II Samuel 11:22.

cal basis and universal legitimacy. As in the Greek epics, myths of the gods constantly accompany and determine all the vicissitudes of the human characters. Nevertheless the *Aeneid* is governed from the outset by a single, grandly consistent promise to which the gods as well as men are subject. The pivot of the whole action, however, is to be found in a human decision—though one made under divine pressure. Aeneas overcomes his human feelings and abandons Dido for the sake of his destiny. The drama of passion, of the loved woman's doom and her avenging curse, is here represented for the first time as a psychic process, in all its searing force. But at the same time it plants the seed of the Punic Wars, which were to be so crucial for Rome. Ending as they did with the destruction of Carthage, these wars opened the way for Rome's rise to empire. Fate dominates the epic; the gods seem to be merely its instruments.

But let us not forget this: throughout classical antiquity and until the end of the Middle Ages, mythic and hieratic bonds deeply affected everyday life. Men lived in myth, lived its patterns, performed in their lives an *imitatio* of myth. Consequently, literature was saturated with traditional figures of speech, with what were virtual formulae, generally accepted *topoi* or *loci communes*. Narrative managed to free itself from the constraint of these traditions and attain to direct, personally experienced intuitions and untrammeled, vital expression of them only by a very gradual process. This liberation was equivalent to man's release from his entanglement with external powers. It implies a clear confrontation between an inner world of the psyche and a down-to-earth, fully present external world. Only then was the way thrown open to the reality of this earth; only then could man begin to deal with this reality, to penetrate into it.

The first stage of internalization, then, consists in a greater inwardness of outward events. The formulaic mythic elements that governed the narrative from outside no longer rule. The individual psyche opens out and finds expression. We can trace the beginnings of such an opening out in the great epic works, at first only in occasional passages. On the whole, however, the narrative deals with external events, with battles, intrigues, campaigns, wanderings, adventures, and erotic bonds. The latter, too, are mostly reported very briefly and in a straightforward, factual manner. Pure lists, like the catalogue of ships in the *Iliad* and the extensive genealogies in the Bible, take up a good deal of space. What are depicted are chiefly deeds and physical incidents: *gesta*, *gestes*, hence life as expressed in gesture, life as gesture. The visible fact is the dominant reality, and even psychic elements emerge mostly (as in the case of Saul at Endor) from factual happenings.[7]

[7] In Greek tragedy internalization appeared earlier and was considerably more developed than in classical and medieval epic. Man's psychic foundations were plumbed more deeply, stirred more fiercely, expressed more intensely in tragedy. Our modern sensibility expects plot, direct action, in the drama. We might therefore imagine that classical tragedy would have depended upon gesture even more than classical narrative. But exactly the opposite is the case. "Dramatic" though Greek tragedy is, it operates mostly by speeches: lamentations and pleadings, hindsight and premonition, emotional outbursts and insights and vacillation. This would seem to follow from the ritual and scenic limitations of tragedy. Narrative is unrestricted and can indulge to the full in the imaginative representation of events; it is under no direct compulsion to turn inward. In fact, the readers or hearers who follow the story as if experiencing it themselves are probably more interested by the full and vivid recital of the events than by any deep psychological probings.

Classical tragedy, on the other hand, because of its origin in

What the reader or hearer is next offered, besides glorification of memorable acts of heroism, martyrdoms, dangers endured, is novelty itself, the novella. The relation of curious incidents, preferably spiced with eroticism, is meant to stimulate curiosity or excite the imagination. Beginning with the *Milesiaca*, the "Milesian

---

ritual, was restricted to specific forms and milieus. Jacob Burckhardt in his *Griechische Kulturgeschichte* (Stuttgart, 1948-1952), II, 289-290, draws attention to the "limited mobility of the characters, who, appearing padded, buskined, and masked, were capable only of delivering speeches, not of action. . . . As for crudities and horrors, the very worst were presented on the stage. Corpses were frequently displayed, and in *The Choëphori* Agamemnon's bloody robe after his murder. In *The Bacchae* Cadmus brings pieces of Pentheus' corpse onto the stage. . . . We had best disregard idealizing extenuations for the absence of outward action and remember instead that even walking on the cothurnus was a dangerous business. . . . The Greeks therefore shifted their interest from the act to the motives; they elaborated the feelings, considerations, and decisions and tried to find a substitute for the absent stage action by narrating the event realistically down to the smallest detail. This function is not relegated only to messengers and heralds. Clytemnestra describes the murder of her husband with appalling precision, even saying that in his death-agony the blood sprayed out like a fine rain, refreshing her as a sprouting field is quickened by Zeus's southwest wind. . . . For depiction of the catastrophe, or even of earlier events—which were usually put into the mouths of messengers or other secondary characters, occasionally into the mouths of the protagonists—the tragedians developed that fiery narrative style so different from the epic style. For the words are addressed to those who took part in the action or who suffered its consequences, and are meant to arouse their strongest emotions. The speaker speaks as an eyewitness."

Thus we see that in tragedy the difficulty of showing direct action, and the determination to have the spectator share in the experience of the drama, produced a degree of psychological change and a concern with detail which the epic achieved only

Tales" of Aristides of Miletus in the second century
A.D., this line continues in the adventurous romance with
a happy ending called the *History of Apollonius of Tyre*
(third century A.D.), and in such Oriental tales as the
Thousand and One Nights, on to the Italian novellas of
the Renaissance, the *Cento novelle antiche*, the stories of

---

much later—had, in fact, scarcely attained by the time of the
Renaissance.

But there is another factor operating. Greek tragedy is the
key arena in which was expressed the revolt of the maturing
individual against the impositions of divine and mythical tribal
powers. And this revolt was not theoretical, as it was for the
pre-Socratics, but very real, springing entirely from personal
experience. That note can be heard most distinctly in the Ores-
teia and the Oedipus plays. Tragedy emerged in the age of a
great transition, in which barbarous savagery (we remember
Clytemnestra's bestial cry of triumph after Agamemnon has
fallen into her trap) mingled with a new, supremely delicate
sensibility and capacity for experience. The concept has been
born of a pure, absolute justice having its origins in this world—
as opposed to the constant intervention of the arbitrary gods.
For the gods, partly guardians of justice and partly highly emotional personalities, reflect the ambiguity of man's condition.
The new attitude is equally at odds with the inexorable law of
blood-vengeance, that rhythm of destiny which forces men to
kill even their spouses and mothers. The free will of responsible
individuals rebels against these compulsions; man, driven into
the corner, caught in the toils of contradictory demands upon
himself, cries out in his anguish, finding new and stirring forms
of expression. And in his search for balance and meaning he
attains to such sublime conceptions of transcendental redemption as in the messenger's account of Oedipus' parting from his
children and his death. Oedipus, having expiated his crimes, vanishes from sight, as if swooped up by spirits from heaven or lov-
ingly received by the underworld: "For he was taken without
lamentation, / Illness or suffering; indeed his end / Was wonderful if mortal's ever was" (*Oedipus at Colonus*, trans. Robert
Fitzgerald [New York, 1941], p. 132).

Boccaccio, Sacchetti, Bandello, Grazzini, and so on. On the whole all of these, whatever their diverse ornamentation, constitute purely anecdotal narratives of the kind we still enjoy hearing on social occasions. Throughout the whole Mediterranean region such tales have always been related by professional storytellers, and in a good many places are told to this day. The "novelty," by the way, usually consists merely in a new variation on traditional forms.

During the Middle Ages, however, Christianity introduced into such storytelling a spiritual and moralistic element of crucial importance to the process of internalization of narrative. In many respects the chivalric epics were already tinged with Christian doctrines. Toward the end of the Middle Ages court culture glided imperceptibly down to the burghers. In the prospering towns the reformist influence of mysticism brought about a merging of the Christian and the burgher spirit. From these sources flowed the moral tales or homilies, and out of these sprang the Renaissance novella, which sometimes shared, sometimes opposed the moralistic burden of the tales. Originally, Christian teachings were explained by exemplary tales, such as the *Dodici conti morali* and the *Fiore di virtù* of Tommaso Gozzadini in the thirteenth century. Later, the story element came to the fore and quite opposite moral observations were often attached to it, as in the work of Sacchetti (fourteenth century). Finally, the stories are freed from their didactic purposes, or express their meaning within themselves. For the most part, that is already the case in Boccaccio's *Decameron* (1348-1353) and in the stories of Cervantes. Yet Cervantes' title, *Novelas ejemplares* (1613) still suggests a didactic origin. But the lessons, where they appear at all, are now merely a pretext;

underneath, the new pleasure in the world and the senses is given free play. In the themes, too, the miraculous and adventurous elements of the past frequently yield to real events in the contemporary world.

In any case, Christian influence left a new residue in narrative: deliberate, imposed meaning. An example of such an effect is contained in the well-known falcon story from the *Decameron* (V, 9). Paul Heyse, the celebrated fabricator of stale novellas, based his "falcon theory" of the novella on it. (Every novella, he argued, should be formed around a point of crystallization, a "falcon.") Boccaccio's story runs as follows: a young nobleman loves a beautiful and virtuous young wife and courts her with gifts, festivals, and resplendent tournaments until he has totally impoverished himself. Aside from a small country estate, which yields him a bare livelihood, he has kept nothing but a precious falcon to which he is deeply attached and which he cannot part with. The young woman persistently refuses him, even after the death of her husband, who leaves great wealth to her and her small son. But one day she unexpectedly calls on her suitor. Overjoyed and not knowing what he can offer her for dinner since he is so poor, he brings himself to sacrifice his last possession, the falcon, and serves it to her at table. After the meal the woman explains the reason for her visit. Her son, who has fallen seriously ill, desires the falcon, and perhaps it alone can save his life. She asks the young man for the falcon, and learns that she has just eaten it. The child dies, but the woman, touched by the sacrifice, succumbs to the young nobleman's entreaties.

What we have in this fine story is the intersection, wonderful, tragic, and ultimately resolving, of affections that move in two different directions. In fact, there are actually three kinds of sacrifice for love: that of the young man, who gives up the falcon; that of the woman, who for the child's sake brings herself to make her plea; and that of the child, who by his longing and his death achieves the union of the lovers. The story is something more than mere "novelty" or curiosity, although it too employs *gesta* and *gestus*. It exemplifies the meaningful and therefore internalizing influence that is under discussion here.

A similar process, incidentally, later takes place in eighteenth-century Germany. There the conventional moralistic tale, Protestant in its origins—I am thinking especially of the *Moralische Erzählungen* (*Moral Tales*) of Sophie Laroche, but also of the influence of Puritan moralism via the novels of Richardson—stimulated Goethe to a new type of storytelling. In the tales inserted into the *Unterhaltungen deutscher Ausgewanderten* (*Entertainments of German Emigrants*), the *Wahlverwandschaften* (*The Elective Affinities*), and his *Novelle* (*Novella*), Goethe conferred a greater depth of individuality and psychology upon this form. In fact, in *The Elective Affinities* he developed the tale into something almost antithetical to its purpose as edification.

In the falcon novella and then in the great stories of the seventeenth and eighteenth centuries—*La Princesse de Clèves* (1678) and *Manon Lescaut* (1731)—psychological expressiveness is no longer a matter of scattered passages; rather, it pervades and embraces the entire narrative. Narration has become entirely a psychological process.

The Renaissance also brought to bear other powerful forces which impelled the process of internalization onward. The age was, like the Hellenistic Age and our own, one in which long-latent impulses broke the bonds previously constraining them. Amid the shattering of dogmas and the transformation of tradition, amid the turbulence of interactions among many human potentialities, a new mode of existence developed.

For our purposes, three consequences of this great transformation are significant, because they were accompanied by a further extension of consciousness into new realms of reality and thus a change in reality itself.

The first is the dawning of, and indeed the political necessity for, individual psychology. When the acceptance of supernatural authority is shaken and each individual begins to act entirely on his own responsibility, then secretiveness, caution, and a close watch on the conduct and character of other individuals become essential. Study of how to handle other human beings leads to psychology. The necessity for self-discipline in the course of protracted intrigues, in the subtle positional battles that mark life in a crowded court, encourages and in fact compels introspection. One's fellow men as well as one's own inner life become objects of conscious observation. In other words, they are objectified. Machiavelli made shockingly explicit what had long been practiced. To a certain extent he legitimized—and that was the shocking element—these practices by bringing them into consciousness. Montaigne initiated the great movement of individual psychology in France. It was still a very casual, wayward psychology; but it was destined to take shape in memoirs and letters, in diplomatic reports (e.g., in the Venetian Relations), and in the epics of the following period much more specifically than in the reflections of Pierre Charron, La Rochefoucauld, La Bruyère, and Vauvenargues. These latter thinkers were still describing types—as did Molière—and their typical behavior, not the individual psyche in all its complexity. A perfect example is Madame de La Fayette's *La Princesse de Clèves*.

This novel, which should be ranked among the classics of world literature, has not received the attention it deserves—at least, not outside of France. In human and stylistic terms, moreover, it is highly instructive. It shows the psychological and spiritual state of French society at the height of the ancien régime, shows it in its glory and in its utmost potentialities. To say this is not to imply that the conditions and human types of the French court are faithfully rendered in any "realistic" sense, or that the behavior of the three principal characters is absolutely representative of a universal point of view (the special sense in which it is will be discussed in a moment). The whole presentation, moreover, is still governed by linguistic and social conventions. For example, all the subsidiary persons as well as the principal characters are depicted as models of beauty, grace, *esprit*, and social art: "Never was there a court with so many beautiful ladies and handsome men; it seemed that nature was taking great delight in showing off the favors that she had so profusely lavished upon these princes and princesses."[8] The action is set in a model environment, and the plot itself is an idealized special case. But the fact that the special case takes the form it does, that the main characters behave as they do, that human relationships at that time could be seen in such a light by a woman who was anything but an innocent, who was on the contrary well

---

[8] "Jamais cour n'a eu tant de belles personnes et d'hommes admirablement bien faits; et il semblait que la nature eût pris plaisir à placer ce qu'elle donne de plus beau dans les plus belles princesses et dans les plus grands princes" (*La Princesse de Clèves* [Paris, 1949], p. 2; translation by Walter J. Cobb [New York, 1961], p. 16).

versed in court maneuvers and an active participant in political intrigues—all this makes the novel so revealing of the psychological state of French society at the time and gives us a sense of what peaks the age had attained. Moreover, beneath the constraint of the conventional façade the real conditions with all their entanglements and nasty cabals are plainly visible. And the protagonists—or rather the victims—of the plot, for all that they are intended as stylized examples, are nevertheless living human beings moving about in real places. The tragic complications in which they become involved, the subtle dialectics of their feelings, the keenness of their decorum—all these bespeak a new psychological insight, and are possible only on the basis of such insight.

The story was written under Louis XIV, but is set in the time of Henry II. The social milieu in which it takes place is described as follows: "Ambition and gallantry were the soul of the court and consumed alike the energies of both men and women. There were so many intrigues, so many different cliques, and the women were so involved in them, that love was often mixed with politics and politics with love. No one was calm or indifferent; everyone was taken up with the business of advancing his own position, by pleasing, by serving, or by harming someone else. Boredom and idleness were unknown. Pleasure and intrigue occupied everyone's attention."[9]

[9] "L'ambition et la galanterie étaient l'âme de cette cour, et occupaient également les hommes et les femmes. Il y avait tant d'intérêts et tant de cabales différentes, et les dames y avaient tant de part que l'amour était toujours mêlé aux affaires et les affaires à l'amour. Personne n'était tranquille ni indifférent: on songeait à s'élever, à plaire, à servir ou à nuire; on ne connaissait ni l'ennui, ni l'oisiveté, et on était toujours occupé des plaisirs ou des intrigues" (*La Princesse de Clèves*, pp. 15-16; Cobb, p. 27).

Let us compare the complementary description of court life by La Bruyère: "Life at court is a serious, grim, demanding game. You have to bring your guns and batteries into position, to conceive and pursue a plan, to counter the opponent's, sometimes to risk your life wantonly."[10]

What superlative, lightning adroitness—and is this not the definition of elegance?—is needed to hold one's own in such a society, and what training in self-discipline this jesting was. Such jests, as Goethe well knew, could be very serious indeed.

The story of Madame de Clèves deals with the passion of a virtuous woman caught between two loves. To her generous and sensitive husband she means life itself—for he dies when he feels that he has lost her. And she herself is deeply moved by his love. But the man she really loves is the Duc de Nemours, whose love for her is as intense and devoted as her husband's. The story is a texture of erotic entanglements among noble and finely constituted human beings. The husband is no cuckold, nor is he a mere spouse who might be satisfied with his formal rights. The lover is no mere trifler; he is wholly serious about his feelings. And the woman is a virtuous wife who refuses to yield to her passion to the very end, even after her husband's death.

Virtue in this story is not just a matter of outward show. It is inward; outward and inward attitudes are one and the same. What is involved is not simply the maintaining of outer forms, the *dehors*, nor convention, and certainly not religious commandments. Religion plays

[10] "La vie de la cour est un jeu sérieux, mélancolique, qui applique; il faut arranger ses pièces et ses batteries, avoir un dessein, le suivre, parer celui de son adversaire, hasarder quelquefois et jouer de caprice . . ." (*Caractères* [Paris, 1932], Chap. "De la cour," p. 278).

not the slightest part in the story; it is not even mentioned. This Cartesian conflict revolves around the preservation of *raison*, and reason in this sense is equivalent to human dignity. Outward forms are of preeminent importance only in this sense, the sense of dignity. And the psychological tragedy takes place in a milieu in which even the slightest hint of emotion, the most oblique betrayal of it, would imperil this dignity. Monsieur de Clèves asks his wife, who refuses to see the man she loves: "Why need you fear his presence? Why do you let him see that you fear seeing him? . . . Why must you be harsh with him? Coming from a person like you, Madame, everything but indifference is indeed a favor."[11]

The obstacles of court society, with the concealments and constraints it imposes, significantly affect the evolution of emotional expression and self-observation. They require and elicit extreme delicacy in the manifestations of love—reversed tokens, sprung from the need for guardedness—and a constant cultivation of emotion. In our own open world, in which all barriers have been let down, such refinements have been wholly lost. Today it is forgotten that the most beautiful aspect of love is not its fulfillment—however intensely that is, naturally, desired—but its growth: the delays, aberrations, slow approaches, the sublime joys that can spring only from suffering. This whole process has been lost to us, since the external obstacles have fallen away.

Moreover, a change takes place in the nature of psychological observation. In the initial stages it was directed toward the interplay between the lovers and the demands

[11] " 'Pourquoi faut-il que vous craignez sa vue? Pourquoi lui laissez-vous voir que vous le craignez? . . . Pourquoi faut-il que vous ayez des rigueurs pour lui? D'une personne comme vous, Madame, tout est des faveurs hors l'indifférence' " (*La Princesse de Clèves*, p. 164; Cobb, p. 148).

of etiquette. In fact, the whole art of psychological observation grew out of that interplay. But later on, as we shall see, observation is directed more and more toward the observer's self, is developed into an ever more probing self-analysis. Thus the outer world becomes included within inner space, becomes in fact a part of the expanded psyche.

The paradoxical situation in which the three lovers of this novel are caught begets emotional paradoxes which are spelled out clearly. Of Madame de Clèves we read: "In [her lover's] presence she could not help but feel a certain pleasant anguish. When he was not there, the thought that his presence could ignite her affection almost made her believe she hated him."[12] Chatting with a group at court, within earshot of Madame de Clèves, Monsieur de Nemours makes the following general observation:

"There are women to whom a man dares not give any tokens of the passion he feels for her except by means of things that do not concern her. Not daring to show her his love, he at least wants to make clear that he does not wish to be loved by anyone else. . . . Even greater proof of a true affection is for a man to change completely into the opposite of what he has been, to cease to have ambitions or pleasures after having been concerned with these all his life hitherto."

Madame de Clèves realized at once that these words were aimed at her. It seemed to her that she ought to reply to them and not condone them. [This for her husband's sake?] She felt she should not be listening,

[12] "Elle ne pouvait s'empêcher d'être troublée de sa vue, et d'avoir pourtant du plaisir à le voir; mais quand elle ne le voyait plus et qu'elle pensait que ce charme qu'elle trouvait dans sa vue était le commencement des passions, il s'en fallait peu qu'elle ne crût le haïr . . ." (*La Princesse de Clèves*, p. 49; Cobb, p. 54).

should not show that she applied the words to herself. [This also for the sake of her standing in society.] She thought she ought to speak and thought she ought to say nothing. What he said pleased and offended her almost to the same degree.[13]

The paradoxicalness of the situation leads even further, and the actual tragedy of these three persons arises out of it. For it becomes evident that in such a predicament preserving one's dignity outwardly is not compatible with preserving it inwardly. Outward dignity demands dissimulation, but inner dignity the truth. The fateful outcome arises from the clash of these two requirements. Madame de Clèves's husband, troubled by dim intimations, presses her to tell him why she is avoiding the society of the court. She decides to make a candid confession of her love—without giving the name of her lover. But this demonstration of her honorable character, this testimony to her inner fidelity to her husband, only increases his love and despair. The confession has entangled her in even worse conflicts. Monsieur de Clèves says to his wife: " 'I feel all at once the jealousy of a husband and of a lover; but it is impossible to feel

---

[13] " 'Il y a des personnes à qui on n'ose donner d'autres marques de la passion qu'on a pour elles que par les choses qui ne les regardent point; et, n'osant leur faire paraître qu'on les aime, on voudrait du moins qu'elles vissent que l'on ne veut être aimé de personne. . . . Et ce qui marque encore mieux un véritable attachement, c'est de devenir entièrement opposé à ce que l'on était, et de n'avoir plus d'ambition ni de plaisir, après avoir été toute sa vie occupé de l'un et de l'autre.' Mme de Clèves entendait aisément la part qu'elle avait à ces paroles. Il lui semblait qu'elle devait y répondre et ne les pas souffrir. Il lui semblait aussi qu'elle ne devait pas les entendre, ni témoigner qu'elle les prît pour elle. Elle croyait devoir parler et croyait ne devoir rien dire. Le discours de M. de Nemours lui plaisait et l'offensait quasi également . . ." (*La Princesse de Clèves*, pp. 72-73).

that of a husband after an action such as yours. . . . You are making me unhappy by the greatest proof of fidelity that ever a woman gave her husband.' "[14]

Afterwards, reflecting upon her confession, Madame de Clèves is horrified to realize that by telling the truth she has "deprived herself of her husband's heart and esteem and dug for herself a bottomless pit from which she would never escape."[15]

And this is in fact what has happened. Events take their course with cruel logic, speeded by the magic of emotions. Monsieur de Nemours, hunting in the vicinity of the Princesse de Clèves's country estate, cannot resist the temptation to enjoy a stolen glimpse of his beloved. Forced to hide, he involuntarily becomes a secret witness of the decisive conversation between husband and wife. Now he has heard from her lips that she passionately loves some man at court, and from certain extremely discreet nuances in her behavior, he can deduce that he himself is the one she loves. Although he "loves too much to confess his love," he is so overjoyed that he cannot resist telling his closest friend about the unusual confession of an unnamed woman who supposedly means nothing to him. But through this friend, the story makes the rounds of the court. It is discussed in the presence of Madame de Clèves and with dangerous references to the source. Monsieur de Nemours, barely "master of his face," nevertheless manages with virtuoso presence of mind to cover up the critical point. But what abysses of

[14] " 'J'ai tout ensemble la jalousie d'un mari et celle d'un amant; mais il est impossible d'avoir celle d'un mari après un procédé comme le vôtre. . . . Vous me rendez malheureux par la plus grande marque de fidélité que jamais une femme ait donnée à son mari' " (*La Princesse de Clèves*, pp. 127-128).

[15] "Elle trouva qu'elle s'était ôté elle-même le coeur et l'estime de son mari et qu'elle s'était creusé un abîme dont elle ne sortirait jamais" (*La Princesse de Clèves*, p. 130).

anxiety and despair open within the lonely souls of the two lovers, who must hide their contradictory feelings from each other as well as from the company. Madame de Clèves, who does not know her intimate confession has been overheard, must reluctantly assume that her husband was the source of the story. And Monsieur de Nemours, ashamed, fearful of losing the trust of the woman he loves, and hoping to injure his rival, reinforces her suspicions of her husband. All of this takes place in the course of a series of general remarks.

Madame de Clèves then bitterly reproaches her husband for disclosing the secret. But he, knowing himself innocent, makes her charges rebound upon herself. In the course of these recriminations she involuntarily betrays the name of the man she loves, which her husband has tried to learn ever since her confession. The mutual accusations widen the gulf between her husband and herself. What is more, the lover who has spread the story necessarily appears to her in a dubious light also. And he, knowing this, is tormented. All three are in a state of extreme emotional confusion. Monsieur de Clèves says to his wife:

"You were wrong. You expected of me things as impossible as I expected from you. How could you hope me to be reasonable? Had you forgotten that I was in love with you, that I was your husband? One of the two would be enough—but both together impossible! . . . I have only violent and uncertain emotions of which I am no longer in control. I feel no longer worthy of you; you seem no longer worthy of me. I adore you, I hate you, I offend you, I ask your forgiveness, I admire you, I am ashamed of my admiration."[16]

[16] " 'Vous vous êtes trompée; vous avez attendu de moi des choses aussi impossibles que celles que j'attendais de vous. Comment pouviez-vous espérer que je conservasse de la raison? Vous

On the other hand the lover, Monsieur de Nemours, could not recall Madame de Clèves's embarrassment and sore affliction without a sense of deep remorse.

All he could wish for was a conversation with her, and even this he dreaded.

"What would I have to say to her? . . . Should I make her see that I know she loves me—I who have never even dared to avow that I love her? Shall I begin to talk openly to her of my passion in order to appear to her as a man become emboldened by his hopes? Can I even think of approaching her? Would I dare embarrass her with my presence? . . . By my own stupidity I have given her more reasons to shun me than all those excuses she was looking for and perhaps would not have found. By my foolhardiness I have lost the happiness and honor of being loved by the sweetest and most estimable person in the world. But if I had lost this happiness without causing her such torment, there would be some consolation."[17]

---

aviez donc oublié que je vous aimais éperdument et que j'étais votre mari? L'un des deux peut porter aux extrémités: que ne peuvent point les deux ensemble? . . . Je n'ai que des sentiments violents et incertains dont je ne suis pas le maître. Je ne me trouve plus digne de vous; vous ne me paraissez plus digne de moi. Je vous adore, je vous hais, je vous offense, je vous demande pardon; je vous admire, j'ai honte de vous admirer' " (*La Princesse de Clèves*, p. 165; Cobb, p. 149).

[17] "Tout ce qu'il eût pu souhaiter eût été une conversation avec elle; mais il trouvait qu'il devait la craindre plutôt que la désirer. 'Qu'aurais-je à lui dire? . . . Lui ferai-je voir que je sais qu'elle m'aime, moi qui n'ai jamais seulement osé lui dire que je l'aimais? Commencerai-je à lui parler ouvertement de ma passion, afin de lui paraître un homme devenu hardi par des espérances? Puis-je penser seulement à l'approcher et oserait-je lui donner l'embarras de soutenir ma vue? . . . Je lui ai donné par ma faute de meilleurs moyens pour se défendre contre moi que tous ceux qu'elle cherchait et qu'elle eût peut-être cherchés

And she herself, caught between the two men, admits to herself with a rush of tears:

> "I have lost the love and esteem of my husband, who should have made me happy. I shall be looked upon by everybody as a person with a mad and violent passion. Monsieur de Nemours knows it now. And to think it was to avoid these misfortunes that I risked all my serenity and even life itself." . . . But however poignant her disappointment may have been, she felt that she could have borne everything if Monsieur de Nemours had not disappointed her.[18]

In such an inflammatory situation, whatever one does goes wrong. Trapped in an inner and outer conflict, tugged this way and that by her lover's wavering self-control, her husband's jealousy, and the world's dangerous scrutiny, Madame de Clèves finds that all her efforts to preserve her honor lead only to further fateful misunderstandings. Finally Monsieur de Clèves, his will to live weakened, succumbs to a fever.

After his death the first frank talk takes place between Madame de Clèves and Monsieur de Nemours. She can-

---

inutilement. Je perds par mon imprudence le bonheur et la gloire d'être aimé de la plus aimable et de la plus estimable personne du monde; mais si j'avais perdu ce bonheur sans qu'elle en eût souffert et sans lui avoir donné une douleur mortelle, ce me serait une consolation . . .'" (*La Princesse de Clèves*, pp. 151-152; Cobb, pp. 136-137, slightly amended).

[18] "'J'ai perdu le coeur et l'estime d'un mari qui devait faire ma félicité. Je serai bientôt regardée de tout le monde comme une personne qui a une folle et violente passion. Celui pour qui je l'ai ne l'ignore plus; et c'est pour éviter ces malheurs que j'ai hasardé tout mon repos et même ma vie.' . . . Mais, quelque douleur dont elle se trouvât accablée, elle sentait bien qu'elle aurait eu la force de les supporter si elle avait été satisfaite de M. de Nemours" (*La Princesse de Clèves*, pp. 150-151; Cobb, p. 136, slightly amended).

didly admits that he had stirred her to "feelings which were unknown before" they met. But she tells him this only to rob him of all hope forever. Although she reveals to him the full extent of her passion, this is the only one of love's sweets that she permits herself to enjoy. The conversation is an amazing one: its intensely moral quality is imbued with flesh and blood, is wholly at one with the finest requirements of sensibility and with a crystalline self-knowledge.

"It is only too true [Madame de Clèves tells Monsieur de Nemours], you were the cause of Monsieur de Clèves's death; suspicions caused by your indiscreet behavior cost him his life just as much as if you had killed him with your own hands. If you had met together [in a duel] in this embarrassing situation and you had killed him, what would be my duty? Yes, in the eyes of the world it is not the same; but in my eyes there is no difference. I know that you and I were the cause of his death."[19]

Nor is this the whole of it. There is still another, extremely feminine motive reflecting the tone of society in that era. Feeling becomes exaggerated to the point of asceticism:

"I know not how to confess to you without shame that the certainty of not being loved any more by you, as

[19] " 'Il n'est que trop véritable que vous êtes cause de la mort de M. de Clèves; les soupçons que lui a donnés votre conduite inconsidérée lui ont coûté la vie, comme si vous la lui aviez ôtée de vos propres mains. Voyez ce que je devrais faire si vous en étiez venus ensemble à ces extrémités et que le même malheur en fût arrivé. Je sais bien que ce n'est pas la même chose à l'égard du monde; mais au mien il n'y a aucune différence, puisque je sais que c'est par vous qu'il est mort et que c'est à cause de moi' " (*La Princesse de Clèves*, p. 195; Cobb, p. 174, slightly amended).

I now am, seems to me such a horror that, had I not these insurmountable reasons for duty, I doubt if I could bring myself to face this unhappiness. . . . Do men in marriage remain forever in love? . . . Monsieur de Clèves was perhaps the only man in the world who was able to remain constant in his love in marriage. . . . Perhaps his passion lasted only because I did not return it. But I cannot use the same ruse to preserve yours. I believe obstacles preserved your love for me."

And then follows an admission that makes her final refusal an ultimate surrender:

"I realize that there is nothing more difficult to do than what I have decided . . . and I mistrust my strength in spite of all the reasons I have advanced. What I owe to Monsieur de Clèves's memory would be a reason too weak if I were not more interested in my own peace of mind. And my peace of mind depends upon duty. Although I have little confidence in myself, I don't think I shall ever overcome my scruples; nor do I hope to overcome the feelings I have for you. It will make me unhappy, but I shall not see you again, whatever suffering it may cost me."[20]

[20] " '. . . je ne saurais vous avouer, sans honte, que la certitude de n'être plus aimée de vous, comme je le suis, me paraît un si horrible malheur que, quand je n'aurais point des raisons de devoir insurmontables, je doute si je pourrais me résoudre à m'exposer à ce malheur. . . . les hommes conservent-ils de la passion dans ces engagements éternels? . . . M. de Clèves était peut-être l'unique homme du monde capable de conserver de l'amour dans le mariage. . . . Peut-être aussi que sa passion n'avait subsisté que parce qu'il n'en aurait pas trouvé en moi. Mais je n'aurais pas le même moyen de conserver la vôtre: je crois même que les obstacles ont fait votre constance. . . . Je sais bien qu'il n'y a rien de plus difficile que ce que j'entreprends . . . ; je me défie de mes forces au milieu de mes raisons. Ce que je crois devoir à la mémoire de M. de Clèves serait faible s'il n'était soutenu par l'interêt de mon repos; et les raisons de mon repos

And after this last meeting she leaves her lover in a state of mingled "ecstasy, mournfulness, astonishment and admiration."

This seventeenth-century novel is far superior to both the moral and the licentious tales of the Renaissance and the early baroque period. In it virtue has acquired a completely new secularized and psychologized significance. Virtue is here not determined by anything external, neither by religion nor convention. The real dangers threatening that virtue are clearly felt and are by no means made light of. Nevertheless virtue survives the challenge with intense self-awareness. The story clearly brings out (and this is why I have described it at length) that urbane and sublimated rivalries in an increasingly concentrated society, accompanied by extreme refinements of self-control, favor the subtlest flowering of emotional life. They are also favorable to self-investigation and self-knowledge. Throughout this novel the psychological states of all three protagonists emerge firmly and clearly. These are still, at this point in the development of narrative, shown chiefly by outer and inner events, rather than by the author's reflecting explicitly upon them and explaining them. But for the first time there is a sharp awareness of such psychological states.

La Princesse de Clèves, we might say, shows us the ideal case of nobility of soul at the peak of the ancien régime. The opposite extreme, the ideal case of evil, is presented in the *Liaisons dangereuses* of Choderlos de Laclos (1782). Here we are shown the degeneration and

---

ont besoin d'être soutenues de celles de mon devoir. Mais, quoique je me défie de moi-même, je crois que je ne vaincrai jamais mes scrupules et je n'espère pas aussi de surmonter l'inclination que j'ai pour vous. Elle me rendra malheureuse et je me priverai de votre vue, quelque violence qu'il m'en coûte'"
(*La Princesse de Clèves*, pp. 197-200; Cobb, pp. 175-178).

perversion of self-control as that regime drew to its close. Stylistically, too, this terrifying book exemplifies a much later stage of narration.

Deliberate presentation of the inner life of both narrator and subjects and of the consequent interacting images and influences involves, we have said, a further expansion of consciousness, a new reaching out of consciousness into reality, and the discovery and inclusion within consciousness of a deeper reality. More or less at the same period, starting with the Renaissance, narrative began to venture into the expanses of the outside world, into the realms of sociality and nature in the wider sense.

The collapse of the Holy Roman Empire and its feudal hierarchy, the collapse of the Roman Catholic Church as a single unified power, and the collapse of the unitary Christian cosmos established by dogma all took place at about the same historical moment. Emperor, pope, and divine ruler of the universe lost their claims to unlimited hegemony. God was displaced by human reason, knowledge derived from faith shattered by empiricism. Men slowly discarded the canon of Aristotle; instead they began themselves to observe nature directly. This was the beginning of natural science. It brought with it a conscious separation of man from nature—an attitude already prepared for by the Christian rejection of the body. Rational man set himself up in opposition to material nature, and in so doing developed a greater awareness of himself. In correspondence to the inner autonomy of *ratio*, the independent world of nature was established outside the human sphere.

Socially, this process was reinforced, toward the end of the Middle Ages, by the rise of the bourgeoisie. Under the aegis of mystical reform movements whose spokesmen regarded Christ and the divine spark as present in every human soul and evident in profane handiwork and everyday tasks, there developed in the newly flourishing towns (especially in the northern parts of Europe) a distinct culture of the bourgeois spirit, the bourgeois spirit of our modern world. In the south, nature had long been humanized and domesticated; it had become a habitation for man. There, moreover, the nobility had early been urbanized and civilized. In the north, however, both nature and the nobles in their craggy castles had preserved a chaotic and primitive cast, a sense of wild untrammeled spaciousness. The crowded towns, tightly organized into guilds, with new administrations, economic orders, and proprieties, grew up in opposition to this primitive spirit.

Out of this sharp contrast between town and nature, burgher and knight, there arose what I should like to call the romantic situation. Nature's primeval wilderness and the colorful life of the knight who adventured through it were objects both of terror and temptation to the bourgeois. A great variety of documents reveal the psychic stress of the burgher. One example is the famous letter of Ulrich von Hutten to the Nuremberg patrician Pirckheimer. Hutten, a knight already infected with the germ of intellectuality, attempts to correct some of the burgher's mistaken notions about the life of the nobility, and to describe the real trials of a knight's life in those times. Another example is Martin Luther's persistent belief in devils and demons; the great leader of the Reformation regarded the elements, lakes, and forests as populated by evil spirits. Still another is the magnificently baleful surge and countersurge of vast intertwined treetops in Altdorfer's paintings of forests—and in general the demonic rendition of nature in German Renaissance art: the Temptations of St. Anthony, the Knight, Death and the Devil, and so on. Finally, we have the embodiment of that bourgeois state of mind in Doctor Faustus, who combines burgher and knight in one person and who, soaring into the realm of the spirit and of spirits, becomes a romantic adventurer in the infinite.

The knight was already obsolescent. He was vanishing from reality, being absorbed into the bureaucratic organization of the new territorial state, which was taking over the whole heritage of the towns, and their administrative methods. But long after his real existence had ceased, the knight survived as a favorite figure in the bourgeois imagination. He became the symbol of the burgher's illicit impulses and wish-fulfillment fantasies. The commercial bulk production of chivalric tales began, in answer to a strong demand. These caricatures of old chivalric epics and forerunners of later adventure stories and picaresque novels, a genre that would encompass the Gothic tales of Walpole and Mrs. Radcliffe, the exotic novels of Romanticism, and the detective fiction of our own time, all have the same function: the discharge of repressed drives.

This new confrontation of man and nature, of burgher and knight, led to significant steps forward in the expansion of consciousness and reality. The new objectifying awareness of nature, complemented by the objectifying awareness of human psychology, produces in epic writing *perspectivistic narrative*, a phenomenon parallel to, though somewhat later in time than, the new perspectivistic painting. Renaissance novellas are still purely linear narratives; they do not reach beyond the mere event, and the locale is scarcely defined. This is true even for the *Princesse de Clèves*, although here the atmosphere of court society is an important component. (But the world of "nature" in which Monsieur de Nemours goes strolling at a moment of passionate emotion is represented by a stereotyped backdrop of weeping willows beside a brook.)

On the other hand, the sensuous reality of the environment is tangibly present in the far freer and more expansive narratives of Cervantes, let alone those of Grimmelshausen and his Austrian successor, Johann Beer (1655-1700). Not that we will find explicit descriptions of landscape and milieu in the works of these men; that comes later. But a sharpened feeling for specific detail breaks through the stereotyped backgrounds. The rise of the bourgeois order, with its marked contrast to the feudal scene, has brought about a new way of looking at the surroundings. Nature and society can no longer be taken for granted and regarded as a unity.

In Greek and Roman antiquity extensive descriptions of sensuous details and characterizations of individuals had already been undertaken. We find them in Homer and in tragedy; we find them as late as Petronius. That is only to be expected, for as a general rule the art of classical antiquity often came to the verge of modern achievements—but stopped short at certain limits. Developmental processes do not proceed in a straight line. Rather, they occur in waves, or, if we prefer a three-dimensional image, in ever-widening spirals. Thus representation of details in classical antiquity bears much the same relation to the modern technique as the "frieze quality" of Greek painting does to perspective, which had its beginnings in the Renaissance. Spatial coherence in the setting, sometimes described quite fully and accurately, can be found in classical works; but space has not yet acquired depth and autonomy. Classical antiquity brought the art of seeing to a high degree of refinement, but much of this was lost due to the medieval suppression of the senses. It remained for the Renaissance, by shattering cosmic and social unity, to open the way for a purely objective vision of nature as otherness. Thereafter that vision could expand without further constraint. The milieu becomes ever more varied and lively. Anticipations of the new way of observing the object already appear in Boccaccio. One example is his description of the plague (in the introduction to the *Decameron*), another is his account of a shipwreck (fourth story, second day). But the new vision first appears full-blown in those works whose narrative centers around contrasts and conflicts of ways of life. In the three great storytellers of the transitional period, Rabelais, Cervantes, and Grimmelshausen, we can see how social criticism in the guise of satire gives rise to a form of realism, that is, more careful attention to the details of phenomena.[21] In Rabelais (*Pantagruel*, 1532; *Gargantua*, 1534) the crude individual satire is still only one ingredient in the rich brew composed of vastly miscellaneous elements derived from

[21] There is a certain connection between this sharpened perception of the material world and particular delight in processes which the later bourgeoisie would consider "indecent": the act of love and the excretory functions. In classical antiquity and in fact well into the Renaissance—in Lucian and Apuleius, for instance, as well as in Chaucer and Boccaccio—erotic incidents were still treated without constraint. There was no hesitation in talking about them, and even where they were deliberately used to lend color to the narrative, the treatment was without the titillating and pornographic cast to be found in later writing. In feudal literature—in Marguerite of Navarre, for example, or Saint-Simon—it is quite natural to include excretory matters in the characterization of situations and persons or in the description of curious incidents (cf. the eleventh story of the second day in the *Heptaméron*). In the bourgeois literature of the baroque period, including the raw satires on military and student life in Germany and the Elizabethan artisans' novels in England, the pure materiality of the point of view is reflected in the crudest descriptions. In Johann Beer's *Das Narrenspital* much is made of farting. Later, as a consequence of Protestant propriety, the narrator's embarrassment about natural processes arises. Decency begets "indecency"; "dirty stories" become the answer to prudery.

many ages and approaches. There are residues of the *chansons de geste*, of folk sagas and fabliaux; there are traces of scholastic tradition, of humanistic versions of classical motifs, and of the religious controversies of the Reformation.

In Grimmelshausen's *Simplicissimus* (1669), too, the world of the senses is not yet distinctly separated from the world of the imagination. As the hero Simplex moves through a world of ferocious war, we are treated to an ever-changing picture, chiefly of the lower depths of society, of a sort still new to literature. Equally new is the bitter and comic manner in which people and places are rendered. And intertwined with this, in a disorderly way, is a full exposition of the hero's inner life, replete with dreams and speculations. In this work, at any rate, the milieu, the background of the narrative, has a power all its own. The story unfolds in a realm that is intensely alive.

In other works of the baroque period a good deal is made of the divergent manners among the classes of feudal society. The story may in essence revolve about these contrasts. Thus *Don Quixote* (1605-1615) is based entirely on the transition between the chivalric and the bourgeois world. The open confrontation between a romantic imagination and Sancho Panza's rough-and-ready reality of peasant girls, barbers, and muleteers produces that double irony which is directed as much against the deluded knight as against the victorious but inferior world of reality.

Two important novels of seventeenth-century France aim their satiric thrust against the rising bourgeoisie. These are the *Roman comique* by Paul Scarron[22] (1651)

[22] On the antecedents and beginnings of the *roman comique*, cf. Henri D'Alméras, *Le roman comique de Scarron*, Les grands événements littéraires (Paris, 1931), p. 95. Charles Sorel, author

and the *Roman bourgeois* by Antoine Furetière (1666).
Scarron started out as part of the reaction against the
chivalric romance and the courtly pastoral romance. Subsequently, he was influenced by the Spanish picaresque
novel, and probably by *Don Quixote* itself. His bourgeois citizens of Le Mans are contrasted not with the nobility, but with a loose-living troupe of itinerant actors.
His narrative remains a semiromantic adventure novel in
which a motley crew of types drawn from the people
frolic amid a variety of scenes in the provinces. Among
their number are comedians, confidence men, ridiculous
poets, swindlers, shady law officers, bourgeois officials,
and provincial aesthetes. The story is shaped partly by
whim, partly by the requirements of entertainment.
Scarron's bantering art of characterization shows through
almost by accident, it would seem.

Furetière, on the other hand, goes about his satire of
the bourgeoisie in a wholly deliberate and purposeful
manner. His work clearly demonstrates the degree to
which a rancorous vision sharpens observation. "Furetière's novel," writes Charles Asselineau, Baudelaire's
friend, "that precise and lively description of the customs
and perversities of an entire social class, is a tableau. It
is the first novel of observation that French literature
produced. . . . To depict, and to depict in caricature, is

---

of parodies of the chivalric and pastoral novels whose debt to
Cervantes is obvious (*Vrai histoire comique de Francion*, 1623;
Le berger extravagant, 1627, later entitled *L'anti-roman*), commented on the new genre: "Good comic and satiric romances
seem to be better reflections of facts than any others. Because
the ordinary acts of life are their object, it is easier to recognize
truth in them" ("Les bons romans comiques et satyriques sem-
blent plûtot être des images de l'histoire que tous les autres. Les
actions communes de la vie étant leur objet, il est plus facile
d'y rencontrer de la vérité").

the novel's basic intention. . . . Never before had the bourgeoisie, with its manners and habits, been the object of such assiduous and detailed analysis."[23]

This novel, too, lacks inner coherence. It does not really have an artistic structure like the *Princesse de Clèves*. What it does offer is an excellent depiction of settings and a penetrating grasp of individuals and of social attitudes. Here, for example, is a comparison between the bourgeois and the noble attitudes toward marriage:

> . . . it is the general fault of girls of this [the bourgeois] class that they imagine a man is in love with them as soon as he has expressed some small courtesy. If he is actually in love they expect him to rush to the notary or the priest in order to vouch for the honesty of his passion. They know nothing of the pleasures of those tender friendships and understandings which beguile the days of our youth and can be combined with a state of strictest purity. They do not consider the good or bad qualities of those who offer them their services, nor do they let their feelings undergo the normal progress from esteem to friendship or to love. Their fear of becoming old maids makes them press immediately for solidity, and they blindly take the first man who presents himself. That is also the reason for the great difference between the courtiers and the bourgeoisie; for the nobles, who make a cult of gallantry and who are accustomed from earliest youth to the society of women, are schooled in courtesy and address. Thereafter they retain these qualities forever, whereas the bourgeoisie can never acquire handsome deportment because they do not study the art of pleasing, which can be learned only in association with women and only after the experience of a noble passion. When the bourgeois

[23] Preface to Antoine Furetière, *Le roman bourgeois* (Paris, 1854), pp. 15-16, 19.

love, they do so only in passing and in an artificial pose, since in fact their sole aim is to marry quickly.[24]

And here—even more significant—is the description of an individual, the attorney Vollichon:

He was a small, stocky, graying man, the same age as his cap. He had aged along with that oily, crushed cap which had covered more wickedness than a hundred other heads under a hundred other caps could have contained. For the tricks of twisting the law had taken possession of this little man's body the way a demon seizes the body of a man possessed. People were doubtless unjust when they called him a damned soul; rather he should have been called a damning soul, for he fastened a curse upon all who had anything to do with him, his clients as well as his opponents. His mouth gaped wide, which is no small advantage to a person whose employment consists in shouting and railing, and for whom being tough of jawbone is a prime qualification. His eyes were shrewd and alert; his hearing was excellent, for he could hear the tinkle of a louis at five hundred paces; and his mind was sharp as long as doing good was not at issue. . . . He eyed the property of others as a cat eyes a bird in a cage while leaping around it, trying to strike at it with its paws. Not that he would not sometimes put on a show of generosity. If some poor person fell into his clutches, a man who knew nothing about legal affairs, he would readily write out a document for him, assuring him that he wanted no pay for it; but then he charged him more for filing it in court than the executor's fees and his own together.[25]

Though the characterization is still highly stylized, a passage of this sort goes a long way beyond the dim, conventional labeling of persons in earlier narratives.

[24] *Le roman bourgeois*, p. 39. [25] *Ibid.*, pp. 44-45.

In England the same development had begun two centuries earlier. It was inaugurated by the phenomenal Geoffrey Chaucer (1340?-1400), a burgess by birth who early moved up in the world to serve the nobility and the court. Soldier, diplomat, merchant, and authentic humanist, Chaucer was adept in a variety of affairs, familiar with several countries. He was a younger contemporary of Petrarch and Boccaccio, and learned a good deal from both. But alongside the descriptive art of his *Canterbury Tales*, that of the *Decameron*—with which it is often compared—seems pallid and shallow, like something out of a different era. Boccaccio's narrative is terse, better formed, more cultivated; it has an even, measured tone. Chaucer's storytelling bursts all barriers; it is sprawling, awkward, loquacious with a bubbling, folksy eloquence, chockful of sententiousness and all sorts of random information. But a new liveliness of the senses, a novel sensuality, an uninhibited delight in living that overflows into visual excitement allows Chaucer to achieve a sharpness of perception and sometimes a striking pithiness of expression that is far ahead of his age. His virtues lie not so much in the narration itself as in the characterization of individuals, conditions, situations. The annual pilgrimage to Canterbury in the spring—an occasion more for pleasure than for edification—brings together representatives of diverse classes and occupations. These persons are delineated in three different modes. In the Prologue, Chaucer introduces them with brief descriptions. Then they reveal themselves by telling about their lives, or in the interplay of dialogue. Finally, they are characterized by the stories they tell to entertain one another. The motifs of these tales are borrowed from all sorts of literary, historical, and mythical traditions. Primarily, these people are types of their classes, conditioned by their origins, situations, and activities. Sometimes they are types of given ages or traits. But individual traits, obviously drawn from Chaucer's own experience, break through the framework of type. In the portraits of these persons the nobility comes off best, of course. The spiciest and most vigorous characterizations, such as those of the various parsons, the steward, the merchant, the miller, and the famous Wife of Bath, are laced with satire. I shall cite two examples, a description of an individual, from the Prologue, and a passage from the Prologue to the Wife of Bath's tale.[26]

> A somnour was ther with us in that place,
> That hadde a fyr-reed cherubinnes face,
> For sawcefleem he was, with eyen narwe.
> As hoot he was, and lecherous, as a sparwe;
> With scalled browes blake, and piled berd;
> Of his visage children were aferd.
>
> .   .   .   .
>
> He was a gentil harlot and a kinde;
> A bettre felawe sholde men nought finde.
> He wolde suffre, for a quart of wyn,
> A good felawe to have his concubyn
> A twelf-month, and excuse him atte fulle:
> Ful prively a finch eek coude he pulle.
> And if he fond o-wher a good felawe,
> He wolde techen him to have non awe,
> In swich cas, of the erchedeknes curs,
> But-if a mannes soule were in his purs;
> For in his purs he sholde y-punisshed be.
> "Purs is the erchedeknes helle," seyde he.
>
> (ll. 623-630, 649-660)

[26] Text quoted from *The Complete Works of Geoffrey Chaucer*, ed. Rev. Walter W. Skeat (Oxford, 1923), pp. 427, 571.

My fourthe housbonde was a revelour,
This is to seyn, he hadde a paramour;
And I was yong and ful of ragerye,
Stiborn and strong, and joly as a pye.
Wel coude I daunce to an harpe smale,
And singe y-wis, as any nightingale,
Whan I had dronke a draughte of swete wyn.
Metellius, the foule cherl, the swyn,
That with a staf birafte his wyf hir lyf,
For she drank wyn, thogh I hadde been his wyf,
He sholde nat han daunted me fro drinke;
And, after wyn, on Venus moste I thinke:
For al so siker as cold engendreth hayl,
A likerous mouth moste han a likerous tayl.
In womman vinolent is no defence,
This knowen lechours by experience.
  But, lord Crist! whan that it remembreth me
Up-on my yowthe, and on my jolitee,
It tikleth me aboute myn herte rote.
Unto this day it dooth myn herte bote
That I have had my world as in my tyme.
But age, allas! that al wol envenyme,
Hath me biraft my beautee and my pith;
Lat go, fare-wel, the devel go therwith!
The flour is goon, there is na-more to telle,
The bren, as I best can, now moste I selle;
But yet to be right mery wol I fonde.
Now wol I tellen of my fourthe housbonde.
  I seye, I hadde in herte greet despyt
That he of any other had delyt.
But he was quit, by god and by seint Joce!
I made him of the same wode a croce;
Nat of my body in no foule manere,
But certeinly, I made folk swich chere,
That in his owene grece I made him frye
For angre, and for verray jalousye.
By god, in erthe I was his purgatorie,
For which I hope his soule be in glorie.

For god it woot, he sat ful ofte and song
Whan that his shoo ful bitterly him wrong.
Ther was no wight, save god and he, that wiste,
In many wyse, how sore I him twiste.
He deyde whan I cam fro Jerusalem,
And lyth y-grave under the rode-beem,
Al is his tombe noght so curious
As was the sepulcre of him, Darius,
Which that Appelles wroghte subtilly;
It nis but wast to burie him preciously.
Lat him fare-wel, god yeve his soule reste,
He is now in the grave and in his cheste.

(ll. 453-502)

Up until the eighteenth century Chaucer remained un-
matched in the depth and roundedness of his narrative
art. Those qualities, however, found their way into the
drama, where they reached a high peak of development.
Shakespeare makes nature a demonic element of the plot
(in *King Lear*, say, and in *Macbeth*, the comedies, *A
Winter's Tale, The Tempest*). The bourgeois world is
present in caricature, contrasted with the nobility. And
despite a certain number of factual errors, the atmosphere
of the locale—whether it is Athens, Rome, Venice,
Verona, or Scotland and Denmark—is vividly conveyed.
The Elizabethan novels—Thomas Deloney's *Jack of
Newberie* (1597), *Thomas of Reading* (1600), and *The
Gentle Craft* (1597-1598) and Robert Greene's *Gwy-
donius or the Carde of Fancie* (1584)—are the first social
milieu novels. Their characters are artisans and cottage-
industry entrepreneurs, the newly rich cordwainers and
"carpet knights," the weavers and drapers. The readership for these novels was also drawn from this class. In-
sofar as incidental aspects of the stories throw light on
conditions in these trades and early manufacturing industry, the novels have a limited interest for the sociologist

and economic historian. But the stories themselves are entirely crude and artless. They consist of bawdy japes or pseudohistorical accounts of how the masters of these trades have risen in life. There is no coherence at all; they entirely lack specific characterization and amplitude. The one remarkable feature about them is that they are, this early, written from the viewpoint of the bourgeoisie, with snobbish glances up to the nobility. The most esteemed of these narratives, Thomas Nashe's *The Unfortunate Traveller or the Life of Jacke Wilton* (1594), is merely a bombastic, melodramatic picaresque novel, a motley assortment of adventures strung together by the hero's imaginary encounters with eminent persons and events of the period.

But the social upheaval at the end of the Middle Ages contained another element that would powerfully advance the internalization of narrative.

The chivalric romances represent, so far as I can see, a genre all their own. They testify to a change in social forms and ways of life so abrupt that it is virtually unparalleled in earlier periods. Admittedly, social conditions and men's attitudes have been perpetually changing since the beginnings of history. But none of these changes took place so sharply and radically as the shift from the medieval feudal world to the modern bourgeois world. And the chivalric romances were the vehicle that brought this shift to consciousness.

All earlier narration was, as we have seen, either a glorifying account of mythical heroes, legendary deeds, historical events, or else anecdotes—*anékdota*. The original meaning of that word is: not yet made public, a novelty, a recounting of singular incidents for the sake of their newness and unusualness. The impulse to tell such tales, as well as the interest in them, sprang from sheer curiosity, from the hunger for new things; it was pleasure in the happening as such, without any additional significance. In both mythic and anecdotal narrative the substance of the story and the audience for it belonged to the same sphere. But we need only compare medieval chivalric epics with their degenerate offspring, the chivalric romances, to become aware of a decisive cleavage. The chivalric romances are directed toward a fundamentally different sphere. People continued to enjoy such stories for their adventures and heroic deeds, for the singularity of the events they related. But over and beyond all that, their appeal resided in the knightly way of life, with its atmosphere of glamor and daring. It was the world of chivalry itself which was the real attraction. For the lordly, flamboyant, untrammeled mode of life *contrasted* with the increasing restraints of urban civilization and the bureaucratic stringencies of territorial states.

In this way, the chivalric romances gave their audience more than the thrill of exciting happenings. They transmitted a whole cultural climate, an experience of life which was radically different from the reader's dailiness; and they made him aware, at least half-consciously, that the conditions of life can change utterly and that the social and moral state of man is conditioned by the age.

This innovation, already nascent in the chivalric romances and brought to its full artistic realization in *Don Quixote*, carries with it another new element of even greater import. *For the first time the individual case is more than an individual case; the story of an individual bears a supraindividual significance.* Through the fortunes of a single person, or the picture of an individual situation, the chivalric romance points to the general condition of man. In short, the narrative has become *symbolic.* One can easily see what this means in terms of the internalization of narrative. Something of general human concern has become lodged in the specific story of a given individual. This occurs consciously for the first time in *Don Quixote*.

A natural objection might be made here: Is this so new? Do we not find in the Bible, in Homer, in Virgil, individual destinies that are of general human significance? In fact, is it not the profound humanity of these individual destinies that affects us so strongly? And then there is the complex case of Dante, whose cosmic pilgrimage refers not only to his own fate, but to that of man in general. Aren't all these examples of symbolism?

To answer such justified objections, we must consider in somewhat greater detail the nature and history of symbols.

As our preceding remarks have implied, a symbol is the coincidence, or rather the unity, of something specific and concrete with something that goes beyond specificity and concreteness. What happens in allegory is rather similar, and for that reason the two are often confounded. If we are to understand the nature of symbolism, it is essential to distinguish sharply between symbol and allegory.

A symbol is primarily a concrete individual case which includes something of a general and spiritual nature. Allegory, on the other hand, is something primarily general and abstract which, after its conception, is invested with a specific body. The very etymology of the two words suggests this difference. Symbol comes from *symbállein*, to bring together, to coincide; allegory is derived from *allegorein*, to say differently.

Allegory is a relatively late device. It presupposes fully developed reflection, in fact the beginnings of a separation between mind and body. Thus it begins with Plato. What is called *allegoresis*, in which literary characters are used to project and explain abstract ideas, arose somewhat earlier, in the sixth century B.C. It originated with the first stirrings of philosophy and the pre-Socratic erosion of belief in the gods. In order to justify the Homeric poems the gods were viewed as disguises for spiritual truths and wise insights. Such apologetic interpretation after the fact does not constitute allegory in the proper sense. But it is a step toward Plato's divine forms, in lieu of personal gods. To the extent that Platonic doctrine is a mythologization of ideas, it contains the germ of allegory. It differs from all subsequent, genuine allegory in that the mythologized ideas signify realities, in fact the one true reality, whereas in genuine allegory the fleshing out of abstractions is merely a means of representing them.

What applies to Plato is also true for Philo (born ca. 25 B.C.), the forerunner of Christian theology, whose doctrines conjoin Stoic, Neoplatonic, and Pythagorean thought with Judaism. He presents his ideas in the form of allegoresis; that is, he offers philosophical interpretations and expansions of Biblical history. But whereas the Greek allegorists took a skeptical view of the Homeric gods, Philo regarded Biblical history as true beyond question. What he called the hypostases—the forces that, according to his doctrine, mediate between God and man— are attributes of God (justice, mercy, and so on). At the same time they are also real angels. The chief of them, the archangel, is the *logos*, which is simultaneously divine reason, divine thought, the word of God as efficient cause, but also God's "first son," God's "shadow," and the incarnate paraclete.

Allegory appears full-blown in that vast pagan poem by a fifth-century African scholar, Martianus Capella, which for centuries was used as a compendium of the world's knowledge: *The Marriage of Mercury and Philology*. According to the Neoplatonic system, Mercury, the god of trade and commerce, personifies the *logos*, the word of God and the divine meaning of the world. Philology signifies encyclopedic, all-embracing knowledge. Mercury wishes to marry, and on Apollo's advice he chooses the most learned of maidens, Philology, and raises her up to Olympus. But before she can enter Olympus as a deity she must get rid of the burden of her book-knowledge. She spews it forth, whereupon each of the other disciplines snatches up the portion that interests her—a somewhat unlovely explanation for the genesis of modern science. At the wedding the various disciplines appear as bridesmaids and deliver lectures on their particular subjects. Each of these lectures fills an entire volume. The personification of the several branches of knowledge is carried quite far, in some passages to the point of obscenity.

The great age of allegory, however, began in the Christian Middle Ages, with its emphasis on "spirituality" and condemnation of sensuality. But sensuality slipped in nevertheless, disguised as Christian moral abstractions. In this guise we find it in that basic work of Prudentius (fourth century A.D.), the *Psychomachia*, which describes the struggle between the Christian Virtues and Vices for the Christian's soul. Much later (in the twelfth century) a similar trick is carried off in the *De Planctu Naturae* (*The Complaint of Nature*) and the *Anticlaudianus* of Alan of Lille. These works established a convention which soon spread widely in Europe. In England and France poems on the theme of "dispute of the Soul with the Body" became standard fare during the tenth, eleventh, and twelfth centuries. Thirteenth-century France was graced by the *Songe d'enfer* of Raoul de Houdan (or Houdenc), and the *Roman de la Rose*, whose influence was long-lasting. In Italy there was Giamboni's *Introduzione alle virtù*, Brunetto Latini's *Detto d'amore* and *Tesoretto*, Francesco di Barberino's

Documenti d'amore, and, in the fourteenth century, the *Intelligenza*, probably by Dino Campagni. In England, well into the seventeenth century, Puritan works like John Bunyan's *Pilgrim's Progress* (1678-1684) and *Mr. Badman* (1680) continued to fulfill the special moral and religious function of allegory. And even in our own century Hofmannsthal has made the anachronistic attempt to approach the evils of the contemporary world with the techniques of Christian allegory as exemplified by the English morality plays of the fifteenth century. In *Everyman* and in *The Great World Theatre* we once more see Faith, Good Works, Dame World, and Everyman striding as flesh-and-blood personifications upon a stage resurrected from oblivion.

As opposed to allegory, the use of symbols is age-old. In terms of duration, vitality, and intellectual content, the symbol has a much wider radius than allegory. It is first of all a special form of signification, and resides in any kind of ritual object. It becomes detached from the original images of totems or gods. I say it becomes detached, for originally the totemistic or divine image is the totem or god itself; the divinity is considered to be actually present in it. But once the difference is felt between the image and the essence, once the image becomes a likeness, the token of a deity already somewhat removed, at any rate not always physically present—once that happens, the image becomes a symbol. The host in itself, for example, and the wine in the chalice, are symbols, just as the cross is the symbolic residue of Christ's passion. But transubstantiation in the Mass converts these symbols back to immediate reality, to the body and blood of Christ, that is, to the presence of Christ himself.

This example will point up the basic difference between the hieratic or mythic symbolism of antiquity and modern, wholly psychological symbolism. Ancient symbolism is *descending symbolism*; our modern variety is *ascending symbolism.*

I call the older symbolism "descending" because the signification subsequently becomes detached from a pre-existent reality, from a higher reality that is superior to the signification itself. In that early world, reality is so monumental, so unfragmented, so comprehensive, or rather so unfathomably simple, that it contains an almost inexhaustible abundance of meaning for us. Therein lies its magnificence. The old divine or mythic entities are not primarily singularities that imply something universal. Rather—despite all their particularity—they are in origin universal entities, projections of utterly real tribal units and ancestors. They are sheer, unadorned reality. This is equally true for the Homeric gods and heroes and for the Biblical patriarchs. Even where an authentic individual is involved, as in the case of Jesus as Messiah, as divine messenger or son of God and "son of man," this individual case is meant to be entirely real and not symbolic. Christ is the descent of God to man, God's act of salvation for man. (At the same time he is brother to men made in God's image, and traces his descent from King David.) His suffering in man's stead is meant in entirely real terms, not symbolically. This reality is still preserved in the Mass. Adam and Eve are primarily specific individuals (and still are so in Catholic dogma), the actual first human pair, through whom sin has come into the world by inheritance. It is only by a gradual process that Adam becomes "man" in general and thus symbolically; St. Paul's association of the first with the ultimate man, of the "old Adam" with a purified new man, contributed considerably to this symbolic sense. The Biblical kings and prophets are not invented fictional characters; they are historical figures, though somewhat distorted by the narratives, for narrative always distorts. They were not created for the sake of symbolizing, for the sake of a meaning; they are the actors in real events, or events believed to be real.

There is an elemental simplicity in these characters and their actions. If, nevertheless, we feel that they represent certain universal human attitudes, we are responding to a naïve symbolism of which the authors were unconscious. That symbolism emerges from the narratives *for us*. Basically it is we who extract the symbolic meaning from them with our insight and our empathy; we make the symbolism. The overwhelming latent symbolic content in the epiphany, the acts, and the passion of Christ was first brought out by the post-Pauline theologians. (Similarly, in works of allegoresis, which are partially symbolic—allegoresis is a curious intermediary form—the meanings were subsequently read into the Homeric, Virgilian, and Biblical characters.) Nowadays we see the simple story of the fall of man as a symbolic account of man's becoming human, that is, of the origins of consciousness in freedom of choice, shame, and labor. But for us to be aware of this tremendous inherent symbolism, we have needed all of human experience up to Hegel and Kleist. We may very well discover a symbolic statement about the German people in the mythical personality and destiny of Siegfried; but the myth as such is not intended as symbolic. The symbolism was deduced from the myth much later, on the basis of historical developments. Similarly, Chrétien de Troyes's Perceval legend was originally retold in an altogether naïve fashion from the sources, sagas now unknown. The grail, *gradalis*, was at first a precious platter on which game was handed around at princely tables. Only later did it become a chalice of divine grace and the goal of a quest.

Dante's *Divina Commedia* is a special case: This great poem is symbolically shaped throughout, with supreme artistic awareness which extends to its most minute details. But it, too, is an example of descending symbolism, for the symbolic structure is derived from God, from dogma, and has thus been cast in terms of an absolute and preaccepted reality. The fundamental plan of the symbolic structure is that of the Christian cosmos, through which passes the specific individual, Dante. It is not a question of Dante's expanding his own personal experience into a cosmos, as Goethe did in *Faust*. Rather, his personal fate and the political destinies of his age—in fact the historical destiny of mankind—are incorporated, symbolized, within the suprahistorical dogmatic pattern: man's salvation seen by faith as substantial reality.[27] (This

[27] As Karl Vossler remarks (*Die Göttliche Komödie*, 2nd ed. [Heidelberg, 1925], II, 630f.), Dante deduced "with acute conceptual imagination, the arrangement of his Inferno and Purgatorio from the form and arrangement of Heaven, which for him was scientific fact." The fundamental unit of the *Divina Commedia* is the number three, in keeping with the Trinity. This is expressed in the triad of worlds (Paradise, Purgatory, Inferno) and is embodied in the structural unit of the poem's terza rima, in the three principal cantos (*cantiche*) and thirty-three minor divisions (*canti*). The resultant ninety-nine cantos are brought by the Prologue to one hundred, corresponding to the number of heavenly spheres. "Within its own framework," Vossler says, "that is, where it is applied, Dante's mathematics is strict and consistent. . . . But Dante does not force the matter, does not attempt, for example, to impose the same numerological pattern on heavenly as on infernal regions. On the other hand, there is also certainly nothing capricious here. The reason for such apparent arbitrariness can, ultimately, be looked for only . . . in the poet's heart and beliefs. . . . Behind every unit, behind every number, we feel the religious conviction of the reality . . . of those other worlds so intensely, so consistently, so tenaciously and continually that the poet in the ardor of his visionary faith

is the central difference in approach between the *Divina Commedia* and Balzac's *Comédie Humaine*.) As hieratically and hierarchically descending symbolism, Dante's was, for the first time, many-layered symbolism, corresponding inversely to the complex patterns of epic literature, in which a totally different, ascending symbolism developed in just as many-layered a fashion, as we shall see.

This new ascending symbolism begins magnificently with *Don Quixote*, which in this sense we can call the first modern novel. The new symbolism is ascending because it proceeds not from a supernatural, extrahuman, or prehuman event whose reality is assumed, but because it rises from below, from a purely human natural world, from individual characters and events which from the outset possess only a representative, not an actual, reality. In fact, they have been invented by the artist for the sake of this representation.[28] The intention is to express by means of an individual's story something universally human, the human situation of an age or of a particular realm of living. Such symbolism, in contradistinction to the early type, is wholly created by the artist. Dante's symbolic procedure consists in fitting the variegated patterns of life on this earth to the preexistent divine cosmos, in deriving earthly life from and leading it to that cosmos. But to the creators of the new symbolism there is no preexistence, no premise outside the work itself. The whole symbolic structure is built up by the artist; it is

---

can scarcely distinguish ecclesiastical, dogmatic, and scientific data . . . from his own inventions."

[28] Even where modern writers such as Gide, Thomas Mann, Giraudoux, or Sartre employ classical or mythological materials to illuminate present conditions, they treat their subjects as parables, not as mythic, factual reality.

entirely integrated. *This complete integration is internalization.* Nothing more is imposed upon the narrator by external reality, or handed to him by independent powers. The artist creates the whole compass of his work out of himself.[29]

How does he create it? By invention, in the root sense of the word (from the Latin *invenio*): by finding. The new symbolism calls for a wholly invented story, a "fiction." Imaginary characters experience imaginary destinies which illuminate and symbolize universal human conditions. All great epic writing of modern times, beginning with *Don Quixote*, is necessarily complete fiction, in contrast to all earlier epic writing, in which the fictional elements were mostly incidental adornment, the embroidery about a core of reality. Even anecdote, which is concerned solely with what is odd and new, was in many cases based on some actual event, tricked out, to be sure, with imaginative elements. This is true for the Hellenistic and Italian novella; it is true for Marguerite of Navarre's *Heptaméron*. The artistic epic writing of modern times, on the other hand, is necessarily fictional. For in order to express something of universal human significance by means of an individual story, the

---

[29] Hofmannsthal, in his essay "Shakespeare's Kings and Noblemen," has described the evolution from Dante to Shakespeare in terms of a similar feeling: "Dante's characters are placed in a tremendous architectonic structure. . . . Whereas Shakespeare's characters are guided not by the stars but by themselves; they carry hell, purgatory, and heaven within themselves . . ." ("Die Figuren Dantes sind in eine ungeheure Architektonik hingestellt. . . . Die Gestalten Shakespeares sind nicht nach den Sternen orientiert, sondern nach sich selber; und sie tragen in sich selber Hölle, Fegefeuer und Himmel . . ."; "Shakespeares Könige und Herren," *Gesammelte Werke* [Frankfurt am Main, 1951], Prosa II, 172).

artist must so select and shape characters and situations that they permit the universal meaning to emerge distinctly. "Everything depends on the manner," Novalis says, "on the craft of artistic selection and combination."

On the other hand, the artistic fiction is bound by the symbolic capacity of the individual story, that is, by its capacity to represent happenings of universal significance. The great epoch of artistic fiction, the period in which epic works of art were able to be, and in fact were, constrained to be wholly fictional, was the period from the sixteenth to the nineteenth centuries. This was a time in which individuals—sovereigns and statesmen—represented and governed their nations, in which world history unfolded in the relations and rivalries of absolute monarchs and their ministers and courtiers. It was the great age of monarchic display, characterized by a highly developed feeling for the public act. Every movement of Louis XIV was a public act. It was France, the *sang de France*, that rose from bed in the midst of a crowd of courtiers, took meals, celebrated festivals. The new self-discipline, mentioned earlier, was directly connected with this special feeling for the public act, for *représentation*.

"Representation," in this sense of "standing for" something else, transposed to the art of narration, constituted the new epic symbolism. This symbolism is artistic representation, and the aesthetic value of the modern epic work of art is actually identical with its capacity for representing the human situation, with its symbolic force. All the major novelists of this period, from Madame de La Fayette and Abbé Prévost to the great English writers of the eighteenth century, from Rousseau and Goethe, Jean Paul and the French Romantics, Stendhal, Balzac, Flaubert, Gottfried Keller, Jeremias Gotthelf, and on to the Russians and Scandinavians—all wrote symbolically in this sense. When the writer extends the individual case into the depths of universal humanity, when he presses realms of new reality out of the individual, he is making him symbolic.

Heinrich von Kleist's *Michael Kohlhaas* is the searing story of a simple horsedealer whose obstinate insistence on justice in a personal legal dispute sows conflict throughout the German Empire, shaking the very foundations of the throne. But beyond that, it is the deliberate depiction of a paradox in our human situation: that "excess in a single virtue" can bring on disaster. "His sense of justice"—his excessively personal, purely human, absolutistic sense of justice—"made him a bandit and murderer." In these words the first paragraph sums up the meaning of the whole narrative. (Under our present social conditions the symbolic force of the story would be lost. In fact, it could not possibly happen in the form it does, for Kohlhaas' indignation would degenerate into personal criminality or leak away harmlessly into the judicial machinery with its endless succession of appeals.)

An additional factor adds to the human and political bearing of the story. Schiller, after all, treated of a similar problem in *Die Räuber* (*The Robbers*); his hero, Karl Moor, represents the romantic and emotional attitude toward justice. Kleist applies a Prussian rigidity to the problem. His solution is a kind of mathematical abstraction. At the scaffold the Elector addresses Kohlhaas as follows: "Well, Kohlhaas, today you shall have your justice! Look here: I herewith return to you everything that was taken from you by force at Tronkenburg and which I as your sovereign have been duty-bound to recover for you: horses, kerchief, gulden, linens, even the medical costs for your servant Herse, who fell at

Mühlberg."[30] Wenzel von Tronka, the junker who had wronged Kohlhaas, is sentenced to two years of imprisonment. The junker's men have fed up the purloined horses and "made them honorable" after their degrading period in the knacker's yard. Kohlhaas' sons are dubbed knights. But Kohlhaas himself, in punishment for his breach of the emperor's peace, is beheaded. Thus the story, the individual case, represents—which is to say symbolizes—simultaneously a universally human, a time-bound political, and a specifically Prussian view of life.

Manon Lescaut and Carmen—not the operatic Carmen but Mérimée's piquant, elemental original—represent two fundamental types of feminine mania. The coldly calculating, yet proud and highly sensitive Julien Sorel in Stendhal's *Le rouge et le noir* personifies the social, moral, and psychological transition at the beginning of the nineteenth century. He is a contradictory mixture of romanticism and the business temperament, and consequently his fate must be the same as that of European man during this period. That is, the drive for power stimulated by the example of Napoleon necessarily comes to grief when it encounters the system of petty climbing which the new plutocracy had established for itself. The desire for heroic action is choked off by the entanglements with female jealousy, and ends in an act of individualistic violence.

Balzac's *La Duchesse de Langeais* describes the tragedy resulting from the encounter of extreme masculinity with extreme femininity. The duchess provokes and tests the feelings of the man she loves passionately by carrying on a tormenting game of yielding and refusing. With consummate skill she manipulates the pretexts of religion and manners. The Marquis de Montriveau, a man of soldierly

[30] Kleist, *Sämtliche Werke und Briefe* (Munich, 1961), pp. 101-102.

straightforwardness and childlike shyness, is ultimately
persuaded by a cynical friend to break the woman by
harshness, to "break" her as a wild horse is broken. "Be
as inflexible as the law. . . . Hit hard, and then hit again.
. . . Suffering develops a heart in women of that sort."[31]
Following this advice, the marquis has masked friends
abduct the duchess at a ball and take her to his rooms,
where he frightens her in a number of ways. After telling her cruel truths, he brings her back to the ball, treat-
ing her with icy politeness and ignoring the fact that he
has already mastered her and that she is ready to surrender to him. This is only the beginning of the torture to
which he subjects her. With the greatest self-discipline,
he withdraws completely from her; he ceases to open her
more and more beseeching letters, in which she puts herself totally at his mercy. She wishes to sacrifice everything to him, her pride, her position, her preciously
guarded reputation. In fact she does so; she avows him
publicly one day by having her carriage stand at his
house from early morning until the middle of the after-
noon. At last she has her aged uncle take him a letter,
which he is forced to read. In it she tells him that if he
does not come to her within three hours, she will dis-
appear irrevocably into an unnamed convent. But Montriveau's own psychological rigidity, the extreme tension
of his hard-won firmness, makes him miss the appointed
hour. Through carelessness in which there lingers a note
of his former obstinacy—a conversation that goes on too
long, a fateful slow clock—he arrives too late at his beloved's house, then too late at his own house, where she
has once more waited vainly at the door. She is gone,
and cannot be traced. No longer the worldly coquette,
she has attained true femininity, a new, perfect feminin-

---

[31] Balzac, *La comédie humaine* (Paris, 1966), IV, 83.

ity of utter surrender, but this has led her to renounce
the world. The desperate man, after searching for her
for years, finally discovers her refuge. But although he
arranges a fantastic abduction from the convent, all he
can recover is her corpse.

The two attitudes of ultimate femininity—to resist
overwhelming force and to surrender rapturously to it—
come together and miss contact with the two attitudes of
ultimate masculinity: delicate shyness and brutal power.
The most feminine of women and the most masculine of
men have passed each other by in their love; they have
missed the consummation of their love and thus the fulfillment of their lives. The last sentence of the story
makes the point: "il n'y a que le dernier amour d'une
femme qui satisfasse le premier amour d'un homme" ("it
is only a woman's last love that can satisfy a man's first
love").

Finally, Flaubert's Félicité in *Un coeur simple* is just
any servant, but at the same time she is *the* servant of
the nineteenth century—in fact, she is really the quin-
tessential servant. She is a classic, flesh-and-blood synthesis of those touching, half-free persons who in their
younger years do not possess sufficient attractiveness and
courage for lives of their own and who gradually merge
completely with the lives of their employers. In the daily
habitude of small services they ultimately come to identify themselves with "the family," whose sorrows and
joys they feel as if they were their own, whose children
they love as if they were their own. Their services are
taken for granted, their feeling more or less returned.
But at the end, as recompense for a lifetime's devotion,
there often remains for them no more than to be the sole
confidante of a mistress who has grown old along with
them, for whom they are the last recipients of helpless
complaints, the last source of human warmth. In addi-

tion, there may be some slight relic of their own lives, a nephew instead of a child, the sick and the old they happen to know, and finally an animal upon whom they can lavish their eternal solicitude, their need to serve. Such is the case with Félicité.

In this simple life story, whose course runs so naturally and normally, precise symbolism, intense selectivity, and concentrated artistry on the part of the narrator are nevertheless at work. This can be sensed in the very name Félicité. The name slips in unobtrusively, an old-fashioned, clumsy name, a true servant's or nun's name, and yet it carries with it such a weight of significance, half bitter, half sweet with benediction. The story is one of continual deprivations. One by one, the persons and objects vanish to whom so much arduous service has been rendered daily in the course of monotonous years. The substratum of devotion vanishes, and the sole yield from all those wasted energies is, in the end, the act of serving itself, the person whose life has been given to service. In making this point the story goes far beyond the specific and becomes a symbol of human destiny in general.

The process of becoming such a symbol has already begun with the story of the young girl's pathetic little love affair. Immediately afterwards, she enters the service of Madame Aubert. Thereafter the symbolism rapidly intensifies. Madame Aubert's pampered daughter is sent to boarding school—a half-death which is followed, after her return, by actual death. The son marries and moves away. Félicité's beloved nephew, who was so attached to her, ships out as a sailor and dies in America. Madame Aubert dies; the house is put up for sale, the furniture is removed, and Félicité's small room, her last link with life, may be taken from her at any moment. Even before this her pet has died too, the parrot that had been given

to her mistress by a departing friend and to which
Félicité, with her ever-overflowing love, had become
attached. The ultimate meanings of the story are bound
up with this bird. For the servant has grown deaf, and
even during Madame Aubert's lifetime the parrot com-
municates the mistress's daily commands by screeching
repetitions: "Félicité, la porte, la porte!" Its voice alone
still penetrates to her from the outer world. Moreover,
it is a living token from America, where her nephew
Victor had vanished. And finally, stuffed, disintegrating,
but immortalized as an idol, it merges with the Holy
Ghost in her mind and she addresses her prayers to it.
"Often, when the sun entered through the dormer win-
dow, it struck the bird's glass eye and kindled in it a
great beam of light which sent her into ecstasy." In her
final illness (pneumonia, "comme Madame") her consciousness takes flight in a last vision: "She believed she
saw in the opening heavens a tremendous parrot hover-
ing above her head"—both psychological and spiritual
transcendence.[32] The attentive reader will notice how
Flaubert, this master of "realism," has employed all the
devices of sober factuality to produce a pattern whose
every detail is shot through with symbolism.

These are a few examples of ascending symbolism. In
all these great narratives a purely down-to-earth, self-
contained fictional special case is so selected and so
shaped, so intensified, that it becomes the essence of humanity, presenting a fundamental aspect of human life
as conditioned by a given era, or the human condition of
an era. But this alone does not make these works symbolic. Rather, their symbolic quality inheres in their
capacity to extend the range and horizon of human reality because—imperceptibly at first—they change that

[32] *Trois contes* (Paris, 1903), pp. 88, 79.

reality. They create a new form of reality, with which consciousness thereafter has to deal. Their artistic act is simultaneously a human act fraught with tremendous consequences.

With this modern ascending symbolism, which in itself constitutes a crucial internalization of narrative, there begins a development that leads to an ever more embracing consciousness and an ever denser concentration, ever richer integration of the content of the universe that consciousness is striving to grasp.

In Part I we have analyzed the early stages in the process of the internalization of narrative and have traced three principal dimensions in which the extension of consciousness and the inclusion of reality move: the depth of the psyche, the breadth of the realm of the senses, and the height of ascending symbolism. All such extensions of consciousness had their beginnings in the first centuries of the modern era, but were not yet clearly developed. From the eighteenth century on they began to be more sharply defined and differentiated.

In considering the reciprocal creation of consciousness and reality, it is difficult to gauge what share the arts in particular have had in changing reality. The same process of reciprocal effects takes place in several fields: between historical event and historical consciousness (a question which deserves special study); between philosophical, political, and socio-economic theories and the corresponding realities; and of course in the natural sciences, where change in the real environment shows up most distinctly, although these changes are not necessarily the most profound. All these elements coalesce and affect each other.

The dynamics of this total process is itself an example of such a reciprocal transformation. In ancient Greece the actual happening which takes place in the *gesta*, that is to say, in the tangible physical realm, is still clearly distinguishable from the mental conception. Man has liberated himself from his primordial entanglement with mythic powers. And although his actions are still more or less religiously determined—that is still true for Plato and Aristotle and the Stoics—he has nevertheless become, in increasing measure, a creature of the earth. He has become himself. In fact, this clear separation and first emancipation is the fundamental theme of Greek tragedy, where man is shown struggling for his moral autonomy, and of Greek philosophy, wherein the shift is made from the divinity of mythic beings to primal substances, mental images, and "world souls." Once such a mentality, independent of myth and religion, has taken form, all political, historical, scientific, socio-economic, and other such concerns are closely and philosophically united within it. And the reciprocity can easily be measured in the relationship between the operative consciousness and the real *gesta*. Let us recall what effects pre-Socratic atheistic tendencies, transmitted by the Sophists, had upon the Greek commonwealths; and vice versa, what influence political conditions had upon the ideas of Plato, Aristotle, and the Stoics. Then, in turn, came the repercussions of Stoicism upon political developments. The reciprocal process can be studied particularly well in the case of such Greek historians as Thucydides and Polybius, whose active participation in political events prompted them to write chronicles. The historical consciousness initiated or expanded by these writings in turn exerted an influence on subsequent events.

In the sectarian struggles within Christianity, and even within waning Judaism, and during the conflicts with the heretics of the Middle Ages, the character of reality changed to the extent that the *gesta*, which had hitherto been pure struggles for power, now became permeated with ideology. Henceforth the intellectual concepts determining these *gesta* no longer seem to come from outside. Rather, the dogmatic tenets are now incorporated in the events themselves, can no longer be separated from these events. (We can see this happening with crystalline clarity in the events that led to the Reformation and in the religious wars of the sixteenth and seventeenth centuries.)

The reciprocal process continues between this dogmatically determined physical reality and the concepts of consciousness. The direct result of the Crusades is a relativization of the doctrines of religion. The indirect result—by way of revival of trade, the hegemony of economic interests and the rise of the middle class, the adaptation of Christian doctrine to the craft attitudes of the northern cities—is a mystical pantheistic extension of the concept of God: the beginning of secularization. The Arabs, in conquering Spain, bring with them the knowledge of all of Aristotle and other works of the classical tradition. This body of thinking, augmented by Arab and Jewish interpretations, further encourages the rationalistic and empiricistic revolt against dogma. In turn, that revolt furthers the transformation of reality during the Renaissance.

For the first time, then, the actual process of change is drenched with ideas, permeated by the products of consciousness. And the shattering of an all-embracing dogma has produced a crucial change in consciousness itself. The secular notions of philosophical minds do not serve the same purpose as dogma; the old cohesiveness is gone. Consciousness scatters into separate fields, and during the centuries of the modern era these disciplines more and more develop into walled-off specialties supercharged with the results of empirical research. Analytical thinking advances in all fields. In its train, the growth of philosophical and scientific abstraction steadily increases the separation of various human activities. Moreover, the systematization and practical application of scientific results—which is to say, technology—strews abstractions throughout the whole field of reality. And abstractions, of course, are the products of consciousness. Then, in the nineteenth and twentieth centuries, the *gesta*—political and economic actions—spread out into complex collective events. Here and there, surface eruptions show the underground presence of protracted processes and developments which are gradually forcing their way out. Conditions become far more important than actions; dealing with them in a practical way demands abstraction. One aspect of all this is of vital importance for our study and must be kept in mind throughout the following discussion. It is that the stuff which becomes the object of the artistic consciousness, and thus of the narrator's consciousness—the sheer raw material of reality—is no longer a merely physical or even psychological primal substance. Rather—regarded from the point of view of its original condition—it is a secondary or even a tertiary plane of life. We might call it a second or third floor. It is a realm already full of a wealth of abstract, "translated" elements, the precipitated salts of consciousness, as it were. Reality, extending upward into realms of life conscious to the point of intellectualism, has become far-reaching and many-layered. All this is the consequence of a general process in which the extension and internalization of narrative played a considerable part.

Consciousness from the end of the seventeenth century on, then, already had to deal with a highly complex reality. More clearly than ever in the past, that reality now encompassed the results of the labors of consciousness. The religious wars were something more than pitched battles among various denominations and doctrines. In them, and in political and economic life as well, theories began to exert a decisive influence upon the course of events. These dynamic theories arose partly out of the new religious doctrines, partly out of the consequences that flowed from the independence of science. The impact of such theories is revealed most dramatically in the birth of political parties in England, and in the French Revolution. During the seventeenth-century religious disputes in England, disputes which were closely connected with political events, the Latitudinarians emerged. Their efforts to mediate conflicts, to simplify and reconcile antagonistic dogmas, led directly to Deism. Deism represented the decisive compromise between religion and scientific reason. Thomas Sprat in his *History of the Royal-Society* (1667; second edition, 1702), speaking of the new scientific association, declares: "they meddle no otherwise with *Divine things* than onely as the *Power*, and *Wisdom*, and *Goodness* of the *Creator*, is display'd in the admirable order, and workmanship of the Creatures" (p. 82). Along with God the soul is also shunned ("forborn"), because to think on such matters leads to talk rather than to scientific work. Consistently, literature is also rejected. In order to purge the spirit of the age from the errors of antiquity "they [the Royal Society] have endeavor'd, to separate the knowledge of *Nature* from the colours of *Rhetorick*, the devices of *Fancy*, or the delightful deceit of *Fables*. . . . They have exacted from all their members, a close, naked, natural way of speaking; positive expressions, clear senses; a native easiness: bringing all things as near the Mathematical plainness, as they can . . ." (pp. 62, 113).

What happened in classical antiquity was repeated during this period, on a broader scale and without restrictions. In Bacon's *De sapientia veterum* (1609) and in Henry Reynolds' *Mythomystes* (1633) we find still another attempt to justify the mythic literature of the ancients by allegoresis. The resultant downgrading of poetry calls to mind Plato's attitude on the subject. Although God is still considered to be included in nature, science tacitly ignores Him. As for the soul, its existence is still to be regarded as axiomatic, its immortality unquestioned; but any further consideration of it is to be postponed until the investigation of material processes has provided us with data which only exact science can supply. Here, at the end of the seventeenth century, we may place the actual birth of modern science and even of positivism.

Yet Deism had another, contrary effect. Although on the one hand it gave sanction to a scientific and exact study of nature, on the other hand it unleashed sentimental deification of nature. The emotions that science banned from its practice and banished from its language found compensatory poetic expression. Religious enthusiasm was poured into nature. Furthering this tendency (especially in Germany) were the pietistic movements, with their antichurch bias and their emphasis on religious subjectivity.

Still another current added its force to that tremendous reshaping of reality that began toward the end of the Middle Ages and reached its maximum in the seventeenth century. Protestantism—which was in every respect a decisive leap toward secularization precisely because of the radical way it internalized religion, making faith a personal obligation—Protestantism detached morality from religion. Thus Luther made morality autonomous by separating man's acting self from his believing self. He made men as political beings subject to secular authority, which he regarded as God's chastening rod. Calvinism accomplished the same end by subjecting man to the probings of his own conscience. Both these doctrines fully accepted the roles into which men were cast by their secular lives and their civil occupations.

In the feudal Middle Ages there had been no such thing as a hard-and-fast, independent morality. Morality was something included within religion and the customs of each class, or rather "estate." So long as Catholicism reigned supreme, what mattered for man was the worship and defense of the Christian God, and obedience to the commandments of the church. By its power of the keys the church relieved the individual believer of the need to justify himself. According to circumstances and very much with respect to persons, the church wielded its power strictly or laxly. Explict morality emerged from middle-class propriety; Protestantism sprang from the marriage of this propriety with heretical mysticism. And the earnestness about morality thus imposed by religion, combined with the inevitable clash between morality and practical necessities, produced those modern psychic conflicts that rack and quicken the inner lives of men.

As a way out of these conflicts, there concurrently developed that collective bourgeois hypocrisy—"cant"— which is found not solely in England. It has become endemic throughout the world. To counteract it, there arose a tradition of moral and social criticism. Such criticism, especially where Anglicanism was hard pressed by Puritanism, took the form of a permanent satirical mood, virtually a satirical condition of life. Most notably in England, the whole of literature was pervaded by a kind of playful sarcasm. The dominant tone was one of supercilious dandyism. It became virtually the mark of the intellectual, stamping his manner and his conversation. (Dandyism is the descendant and the middle-class continuation of the self-mastery practiced by the nobility— an ethic drawn from a variety of sources.) But as bourgeois mores have spread increasingly through the whole of society, dandyism with its virtuoso self-display has moved out to the periphery. The noble dandy stood at the center of a court society and could be considered representative of it. The bourgeois dandy is off-center in the bourgeois world, and provides titillation for that world by shocking it. (Shakespeare's Richard II and Prince Hal are prime examples of the original type from which the dandy traces his lineage. Within bourgeois society he assumes the position, and the limitless sovereignty, of Shakespeare's jesters and clowns.)[1]

As a result of the social and intellectual constellation described above, a further psychological phenomenon arose, once more chiefly, or at least earliest, in England. The Puritan habit of agonizing examination of conscience produced the intense solitude of the Puritan psyche. Ordinary life, more and more dominated by commerce, devalued feeling. Science and Protestantism lent a certain aura of disreputability to expressions of emotion. All these elements combined to create that melancholia, that cultivation of the pleasures of suffering,[2] which was the reverse of the satirical mood. Odes to melancholy and solitude run through all of English poetry from the end of the seventeenth to the begin-

[1] The relationship between the dandy and the clown is touched on in Hugo von Hofmannsthal's *Der Schwierige*. Describing the clown Furlani and his *élégance*, Hofmannsthal's Karl Bühl says: "But what Furlani does is on a much higher level than what all the others do. All the others are following a purposeful line and look neither right nor left, they hardly even breathe till they have achieved their purpose. . . . But he apparently has no purpose of his own. . . . He's wonderful to watch in his lovely nonchalance—but his very nonchalance of course needs twice as much skill as the tension of the others" (*The Difficult Man*, trans. Willa Muir, in *Hugo von Hofmannsthal: Selected Plays and Libretti*, Bollingen Series 33.3 [New York, 1963], pp. 719-720).

[2] *The Pleasures of Melancholy* is the title of a poem by Thomas Warton (written in 1745).

ning of the nineteenth centuries. Repressed emotion was channeled elegiacally into poetry and there mingled with sentimental worship of nature.

Such, then, was the reality of the age. And consciousness, laboring to shape that reality further, was already having to deal with itself, with its own states and products. A new intertwining of inner and outer life began, within the context of a more developed consciousness. As we have seen, early mythical and magic involvement of man with the elemental powers outside him dominated and determined human life. But in the new combination, the growing power and extension of conscious inner life begins to assert itself. In the eighteenth century the process of internalization enters a new stage, which we shall be studying through examples of the changing nature of narrative. The interpenetration of consciousness and reality, and the accelerating interaction between the two, have greatly complicated the problem. To try to follow the process in all its intricacies would be to lose the thread entirely in the synopses of individual works. Since we are concerned primarily with tracing the main outlines of the process, we shall limit ourselves here to setting down the essential results of this new phase in the expansion of consciousness and the change of reality.

Let us note as the primary result that in this period *nature for the first time becomes an independent object of observation.*[3] No longer is it merely the environment within which human movement takes place, or the substratum of human activity, as it was in Virgil's *Georgics* and *Bucolics* and throughout the long tradition of pas-

---

[3] As was the case with the development of perspective, the graphic arts took the lead here. During the Renaissance, Altdorfer and Dürer painted the first landscapes devoid of human figures.

toral poetry, and as it continued to be even in the "perspectivistic" narrative of the Baroque Age. The secularized religious spirit of Deism drew a line between nature and man; henceforth nature was regarded as a manifestation of the divine creation. This attitude was first expressed in poetry, for example in Pope's *Windsor Forest* (1713) and Thomson's *The Seasons* (1726-1730). In Germany it began with Barthold Heinrich Brockes' *Irdisches Vergnügen in Gott* (*Earthly Delight in God*, 1721-1748), written under English influence, and Albrecht von Haller's *Die Alpen* (*The Alps*, 1729).

To be sure, such works were still, in essence, an approach to divine worship via poetry. Nature description in Thomson is highly generalized, without reference to any given locale—as has often been remarked. Concrete observation of natural phenomena is scanted in favor of sentimentalized raptures. Everything is mythical and sprinkled with allegory, the allegorical figures jumbled together with the mythical personages. Pomona, Bacchus, Nature, Beauty, Commerce, Poesy, Philosophy, the Seasons, Britannia, the Thames sound like minor gods, and along with the Creator himself are enthusiastically addressed in classical vocatives:

> Hail, SOURCE OF BEINGS! UNIVERSAL SOUL
> Of Heaven and Earth! ESSENTIAL PRESENCE, hail!
> To THEE I bend the Knee; to THEE my Thoughts,
> Continual, climb. . . .[4]

And similarly: "Come, gentle SPRING, Ethereal Mildness, come. . . ."[5] Or: "With Thee, serene PHILOSOPHY,

[4] *The Seasons*, "Spring," ll. 553-556. The text is from the last edition corrected by the author (London, 1746).
[5] "Spring," l. 1.

with Thee, / And thy bright Garland, let me crown my Song!"[6] Or: ". . . O THAMES, / Large, gentle, deep, majestic, King of Floods!"[7]

Rational speculation and erudition still hold in check the upswell of emotion: "with the Light of thoughtful Reason mix'd, / Shines lively Fancy and the feeling Heart. . . ."[8]

The revolutionary discoveries of physics and astronomy were changing poetic vision and widening its range; and the poems of the time proudly hailed the new sciences (later, in Blake and Keats, resentment against a science antipathetic to poetry would arise). But already we may detect, even in Thomson, a certain nostalgia for the old naïve vision. He contrasts the new abstract analysis of phenomena with the unclouded sensuous pleasures of youth:

> Here, awful NEWTON, the dissolving Clouds
> Form, fronting on the Sun, thy showery Prism;
> And to the sage-instructed Eye unfold
> The various Twine of Light, by thee disclos'd
> From the white mingling Maze. Not so the Swain,
> He wondering views the bright Enchantment bend,
> Delightful, o'er the radiant Fields, and runs
> To catch the falling Glory; but amaz'd
> Beholds th' amusive Arch before him fly,
> Then vanish quite away. . . .[9]

The evocation of landscape, though still couched in terms of classicistic tranquility and harmony, has nevertheless come a long way. It is spontaneous, filled with a fresh, zestful acuity. Here, for example, is an autumnal scene reminiscent of Breughel's paintings of the seasons:

[6] "Summer," ll. 1715-1716.   [7] "Autumn," ll. 124-125.
[8] "Spring," ll. 485-486.   [9] "Spring," ll. 208-217.

. . . Attemper'd Suns arise,
Sweet-beam'd, and shedding oft thro lucid Clouds
A pleasing Calm; while broad, and brown, below
Extensive Harvests hang the heavy Head.
Rich, silent, deep, they stand; for not a Gale
Rolls its light Billows o'er the bending Plain;
A Calm of Plenty! till the ruffled Air
Falls from its Poise, and gives the Breeze to blow.
Rent is the fleecy Mantle of the Sky;
The Clouds fly different; and the sudden Sun
By Fits effulgent gilds th' illumin'd Field,
And black by Fits the Shadows sweep along.
A gayly-checker'd Heart-expanding View,
Far as the circling Eye can shoot around,
Unbounded tossing in a Flood of Corn.[10]

Germany at this same period lacked that background of humanistic classicism English poetry could look to. Yet there too a nature poetry was being written. Compared to its English counterpart, its faults were glaring. The emotional growth of this poetry is smothered before it can begin under a welter of ideas and intentions, a flood of religious didacticism, a mass of factuality from the natural sciences. And since direct emotion is thus blocked, the expressiveness which should emerge from emotional contemplation cannot properly develop. The great poems of the German baroque period are eruptions of repressed emotion, lamentations, desperate plaints on human destiny, wrung from their writers by personal misfortune and the terrible conditions of the times. But as soon as poetry turns to deistic observation of nature, expressiveness is wrecked on reefs of clichés—the clichés of borrowed and warmed-over enthusiasms exaggerated because all their initial heat is gone. Only now and then does a new image appear or an original note make itself heard.

[10] "Autumn," ll. 28-42.

The writers of this period created that dismal bookish German which continued to prevail until the end of the nineteenth century in literature and even in general conversation. Only men with unusual power of feeling managed to break away from that language, which totally lacked the faculty for spontaneity and therefore made do with stale coinages, banal metaphors, worn quotations, and stock jokes. Its blight fell most heavily on poetry, which was in any case grotesquely overloaded with information. (Later the intruder was to be journalism, which, under the necessity of rapidly setting forth and inflating facts, prepackaged rhetorical devices for general consumption.) In France and England, too, the poetry of the seventeenth and eighteenth centuries was filled with scholarly and philosophical matter; but even though such material burdened the language of poetry, it became part of it, was integrated into it. In Germany alone no such mixing took place; learned language remained in unassimilated lumps within the substance of the poems. In Germany alone, therefore, a sharp opposition arose, not between poetry and prose—that exists everywhere—but between "the poetic" and "the prosaic." The distinction did harm to both, for in this radical dichotomy poetry was wrongly exalted above true reality, prose equally wrongly reduced to the most materialistic state of reality.

If we compare Thomson with his German contemporary Brockes, we will see this divergence plainly. Brockes is not without poetic sensibility; quite often he manages to pin down a subtle impression of nature, such as the "changeable green" of the rose beetle, or the visibility of cold, as in the lines from "Wintergedanken" ("Winter Thoughts"):

It seems as though within a hoary Mist
'Tis possible to see the Cold itself.

But immediately afterwards the poetic tone is rudely broken; the poem veers off into a didactic, edifying treatise:

> The Air grows stiff, by icy Frost compacted,
> The River iron-hard, the Earth to Stone contracted,
> Yea, stony indeed. For have we not learned
> Of entire Cities that to Stone were turned,
> And wondered much thereat. But we discerned
> More Wonder herein, not that all we see
> Has changed to such Solidity
> And everything a fearful Stiffness shows,
> But that each of us by Experience knows
> That our Creator, in his Almighty Sway,
> Can soften Stone and melt the Ice away.[11]

By comparison, we must marvel at the evenness with which Thomson preserved the poetic tone in his description of Newton's theory of color. In English poetry, too, nature is often evoked as proof of the skill of the Creator, but the theme is always handled with grandeur. Thus,

[11]

> Es scheint als könne man in einem greisen Duft
> Die Kälte selbst anjetzt ganz sichtbar sehn. . . .

> Die durch den scharfen Frost gepresste Luft erstarrt,
> Die Flut wird eisenfest, die Erde felsenhart,
> Ja felsicht in der That. Wenn man wohl eh gehört,
> Dass ganze Städte sich in Stein verkehrt,
> Erstaunet man darob. Dies ist erstaunenswert,
> Dass nicht nur alles sich fast in der That
> In Stein verwandelt hat
> Und alles was man sieht, ein starres Schreckbild weiset,
> Nein, dass, wie durch Erfahrung ja bekannt,
> Durch unsers Schöpfers Allmachtshand
> Sich alles wiederum entsteinet und enteiset. . . .

(Quotations here and below are from Barthold Heinrich Brockes, *Irdisches Vergnügen in Gott* [Stuttgart, 1963].)

Thomson celebrates the Creator in terms of the cycle of the year. His disciple David Mallet, in his *Winter's Day*, celebrates his feelings for nature in terms of the course of a single day. Even the so-called scientific poets, such as Sir Richard Blackmore or Henry Brooke, know how to display their learning within a graceful framework (*Creation*, 1712; *Universal Beauty*, 1735). But we shall scarcely find, in English poetry, anything so incongruous as an attempt to praise the operations of divinity through contemplation of the structure of a fly.[12] Nor will we find such abstruse notions as that of "rational odor." Among the German poets of the period, the convention itself, in its restrictiveness, forced the writer to expatiate on the most material, minute details. But precisely this unpoetic pedantry produced an unexpected result in Germany: the deistic requirement to celebrate nature was carried beyond the limits set by the English poets. Observation approached closer to the phenomena themselves. Thomson achieves superior form and poetic

[12] Insects have served English poets solely as satirical motifs. Compare, for example, "A comical Panegyrick on that familiar Animal by the Vulgar call'd a Louse, produced by Mr. Willis of St. Mary Hall, Oxon," in *The Works of Mr. Thomas Brown in Prose and Verse* (London, 1707):

> Tremendous Louse, who can withstand thy Power,
> Since Fear, at first, taught Mortals to adore?
>
> . . . .
>
> Who can thy Power describe, thy Glories scan
> Thou Lord of Nature, since thou'rt Lord of Man?
> In these we may thy wondrous value see
> The World was made for Man, and Man for Thee.

The flea is also apostrophized in Donne's arch and witty love poem, "The Flea." By his double bite the flea mingles the blood of the lover with the blood of his over-virtuous sweetheart in a lascivious swelling.

restraint in his nature-painting, but he remains more general and more aloof than Brockes. In the latter, wooden phrases, tiresome cataloguing, and painfully cautious scientific descriptions alternate with tender expressions of real feeling. The following passages are from the poem "Die Nachtigall und derselben Wettstreit gegen einander" ("The Contest of the Nightingale"):[13]

In Springtime was I stirred to my Soul's deepest
   Bounds
By the Queen of the Thickets, the lovely Nightingale,
Who fills the greatest Forests with her wondrous
   Sounds
From a Throat so small and from a Breast so frail.
Her Skill, her Diligence, her Strength and Artistry,
Her Changes, Pitch and Tone are a true Prodigy
Of toiling Nature, who has 'stablished such a strong
Music in scanty Feathers, so pitiable and weak,
And stored such heavy Burdens of enchanting Song
In such diaphanous Skin and such a tender Beak.

. . . .

She peeps, tunes up, and sings with such graceful
   Allure,

13

Im Frühling rührte mir das Innerste der Seelen
Der Büsche Königin, die holde Nachtigall,
Die aus so enger Brust und mit so kleiner Kehlen
Die grössten Wälder füllt durch ihren Wunderschall.
Derselben Fertigkeit, die Kunst, der Fleiss, die Stärke,
Verändrung, Stimm' und Ton sind lauter
   Wunderwerke
Der wirkenden Natur, die solchen starken Klang
In ein paar Federchen, die kaum zu sehen, senket
Und einen das Gehör bezaubernden Gesang
In solche dünne Haut und zarten Schnabel schränket.

. . . .

Sie zwitschert, stimmt und schlägt mit solcher
   Anmut an,

With such an artfully intricate Twittering,
That I am quite dumbfounded nor can say for sure
Whether she sighs while laughing, or laughs while
    chirruping.
Her lovely Voice takes Flight in one long fluted Line
From low to high, then falls, then rises up again,
And hovers in strict Time; then swiftly there combine
Showers of different Notes into refreshing Rain.
She turns, draws out, and breaks, then repeats the
    Strain,
Sings clear, sings harsh, sings soft, she sings with Might
    and Main.
No Arrow flies so swiftly, no Lightning strikes so fast,
Winds cannot rage so fiercely in stormy Overcast,
As when her amiable and singular Melody
Swirls and rings and changes, checks and runs on
    free.

The outcome of all this is that in German deistic poetry, precisely where it is poetically most defective and
precisely because of these defects, consciousness seized

Mit solchem nach der Kunst gekräuseltem Geschwirre,
Dass man darob erstaunt und nicht begreifen kann,
Ob sie nicht seufzend lach', ob sie nicht lachend girre.
Ihr Stimmchen ziehet sich in einer hohlen Länge
Von unten in die Höh, fällt, steigt aufs neu empor,
Und schwebt nach Mass und Zeit; bald drängt sich eine
    Menge
Verschiedner Tön' aus ihr als wie ein Strom hervor.
Sie dreht und dehnt den Ton, zerreisst und fügt ihn
    wieder,
Singt sanft, singt ungestüm, bald klar, bald grob, bald
    hell.
Kein Pfeil verfliegt so rasch, kein Blitz verstreicht so
    schnell,
Die Winde können nicht so streng im Stürmen wehen,
Als ihre schmeichelnde verwunderliche Lieder
Mit wirbelndem Geräusch sich ändern, sich
    verdrehen. . . .

upon the reality of nature to a degree that had not yet been achieved in the contemporary novels. As the apogee of this phase I shall quote the first exact description of a thunderstorm. For all that it veers off here and there into archness or degenerates into verbosity, as a whole and in separate images it nevertheless has grandeur. Here is an abbreviated selection from Brockes's poem "Die auf ein starkes Ungewitter erfolgte Stille" ("The Silence After a Thunderstorm"):[14]

> For thirty Days unbroken the Sun had lately smiled
> Upon a springtime World, with Blossoms newly
>   dressed,
> And everything I saw, with Joy and Ease beguiled,
> Flamed with Brightness that filled Things with Zest.
> Flame flowed through Town and Country, filmed the
>   Lakes and Streams,
> Plunged into Tellus' Womb so deep that in its Beams
> The Fields and Cliffsides glowed, and glistened Sand
>   and Stone.
> The damp Cloudbursts of yore seemed Things
>   well-nigh unknown,
> Until at last upon a sultry midday Hour
> A tiny Cloud appeared, and but a Moment thence
> It seemed to swell. The Air suddenly grew dense.

[14]

> Nachdem die Sonne jüngst seit zweimal fünfzehn
>   Tagen
> Die neu beblümte Welt beständig angelacht,
> Schwamm alles, was man sah, in Wollust und Behagen;
> Die Glut, die alles hell, die alles lebhaft macht,
> Beflosse Stadt und Land, bedeckte See und Flüsse,
> Sie senkte sich so tief in Tellus' Schoss hinein,
> Dass Feld und Felsen glüht'; es glänzte Sand und Stein,
> Man kennete fast nicht die feuchten Wolkengüsse,
> Bis endlich sich einmal bei schwülen Mittagsstunden
> Ein kleines Wölkchen zeigt' und in dem Augenblick
> Sich auszuspannen schien. Die Luft ward plötzlich dick,
> Das Licht ward allgemach vom Schatten überwunden,

The Light succumbed, though slowly, to the Shadow's
    Power.
Into the Sky there rose Fog and Mist and Cloud;
The Gold of Day was bleached, the cheerful Blue
    dispelled,
The dense and turbid Air laid on the Sea a Shroud;
The Brooks looked black, the Rivers brown and sallow,
And out to the Horizon hung heavy Haze and Rain.
No Birds were to be seen except the timid Swallow
That swooped low and alone, forward and back again,
As if in frantic Terror of the threatening Air
It sought in Earth or Water a Refuge to prepare.
Such a Stillness filled and weighed upon the World—
For Fear, not a Weed stirred, nor a Leaf uncurled—
That I in Fright stood rigid and watched with staring
    Eyes.
Nature herself, distorted and taken by Surprise
Seemed terrified as well, and could do naught but wait,
Uncertain, fearful of the threatening Bane—
Until, shatt'ring th' ominous Silence, a Hurricane

Es stiegen Nebel, Duft und Wolken in die Höh',
Des Tages Gold erbleicht', es schwand das heitre Blau,
Die dicke, trübe Luft beschattete die See;
Die Bäche schienen schwarz, die Flüsse braun und
    falbe,
Der ganze Luftkreis ward von Duft und Regen schwer,
Kein Vogel war zu sehn, die auch schon scheue
    Schwalbe
Schoss nur allein, jedoch ganz niedrig, hin und her;
Es liess, als wollte sie in Erd' und Flut, vor Schrecken
Vor dem was in der Luft ihr drohte, sich verstecken.
Solch eine Stille füllt' und druckte recht die Welt,
Dass man, wie sich kein Blatt, kein Kraut vor Schrecken
    rührte,
Vor Furcht selbst unbewegt mit starren Augen spürte.
Es schien selbst die Natur erstaunet und entstellt
Vor Warten und vor Furcht der Dinge,
Die sie bedrohte, bis plötzlich ein Orkan
Die bange Stille brach, so dass der Lüfte Bahn

Burst forth like a rushing River in Spate.
A Whirling filled the Air with Grains of Dust and Sand
As Winds from every Quarter pounced upon the Land.
The Forest seemed an Ocean, with green Waves
  billowing;
The Branches shrieked and howled, their Foliage
  Thundering.
Now the Swell of the lashing Leaves
Is whirled aloft with a rushing Bruit,
Now a sudden downward Tug receives
So that the Crown touches the loosened Root.
Here a massive Branch abruptly cracks and breaks,
There a deeply rooted, ancient Oak Tree crashes.
The Whirlwind from the Twigs a leafy Army shakes
That fly through the gray Air like Cinders from hot
  Ashes.
. . . .
Lightning, Torrents, Jets. The Thunder rolled and
  crashed.

Wie eine wilde Flut schnell an zu rauschen finge.
Von allen Winden ward der Erdkreis überfallen,
Ein Wirbel füllete die Luft mit Sand und Staub,
Es schien der Wald ein Meer, drin grüne Wellen
  wallen,
Die Zweige heulten recht, es brauste das Laub.
Bald wurden der gepeitschten Blätter Wogen
Mit sausendem Geräusch empor geführt,
Bald plötzlich unter sich gezogen,
Dass oft der Wipfel selbst die lose Wurzel rührt'.
Hier borst und brach ein dick belaubter Ast,
Dort kracht und stürzt, von Wirbel aufgefasst,
Ein tief gewurzelter bejahrter Eichbaum nieder.
Der Blätter Heer, von Zweigen abgestreift,
Flog durch die graue Luft wie Kohlen hin und wieder.
. . . .
Der Donner rollt' und knallt', Blitz, Ströme, Strahlen,
  Schlossen

Hailstones added their Wrath; the red Flames flashed,
Surging to and fro like a fiery Sea,
Tearing the very Air and blazing fearfully.
While at the selfsame Moment, in violent Undulation,
Flew whole Streams and Rivers of concentrated Rain,
Which Boreas anon drove in such Agitation
That even the very Shape of Water could not remain.
Bending under the Lash, it veiled the Light of Day
And filled the blackened Air with a sheer white Spray.
A steady Cloudburst poured its drenching Flow
With roaring Noises through the Lightning's glow
Until both howled and hissed; it soaked the parchèd
    Field,
And swallowed up the Grain; an earth-shaking Din
Erupted everywhere; the whole World reeled,
The Mountains swayed; the black Air threw
Its dusky Portals wide; I thought I saw therein
A Maw of Flames and Steam, a Gulf of hellish Brew,

Vermischten ihre Wut, die roten Flammen flossen
Und wallten überall als wie ein feurig Meer
In der geborstnen Luft entsetzlich hin und her,
Worin zu gleicher Zeit mit ungestümen Wogen
Verdickte Regenström' und ganze Flüsse flogen,
Die öfters Boreas so durcheinander trieb,
Dass die Gestalt nicht einst vom Wasser überblieb,
Indem es wie gepeitscht des Tages Licht verhüllte
Und mit ganz weissem Schaum die schwarzen Lüfte
    füllte.
Ein steter Wolkenbruch stürzt' eine dicke Flut
Mit brausendem Geräusch von oben durch die Glut,
Dass beides rauscht' und zischt', beströmt' das trockne
    Feld,
Verschluckte das Getreid'; ein allerschütternd Krachen
Brach allenthalben aus; es zitterte die Welt,
Die Berge wankten recht; es riss die schwarze Luft
Die düstern Pforten auf; sie schien ein weiter Rachen
Voll Flammen, Dampf und Glut, ja eine Höllengruft,

And in that glowing Pit, that vast, unending Rift,
A quivering Host of Beams, dazzlingly bright,
Ran with jagged Motion, now to left, now right,
Now round, now serpentine, and indescribably swift.
Then this Chasm closed so suddenly again,
Striking the stunned Eyelids of all mortal men
With so dense a Darkness and pitchblack a Night
That it could not be said
Whether Light or Shade
Besieged the Heart with greater Fright.
Here Lightning briefly flashes, while there the Heavens
    shake,
For the single bolt makes the Horizon quake.

Still Flash on Flash shone with a fearful Flame,
Still Thunder rumbled with a ghastly roar,
Then, in a Moment, gentle Stillness came,
Wrapping the nigh-stunned World in Peace once
    more.

In deren lichtem Pfuhl und ungeheuren Tiefe
Ein schütternd Strahlenheer, das Licht erschrecklich
    hell,
Bald rund, bald schlangenweis und unbeschreiblich
    schnell
Mit zackichter Bewegung liefe.
Dann schloss sich diese Kluft so plötzlich wieder
Und schlug der Sterblichen erschrockne Augenlider
Mit dicker Dunkelheit und so pechschwarzer Nacht,
Dass es noch ungewiss,
Ob Licht, ob Finsternis
Dem Herzen grössre Furcht gemacht.
Da blitzt es kurz, hier auch, wenn's dorten zehnfach
    wittert,
Weil in dem langen Blitz der ganze Luftkreis zittert.

Noch strahlte Blitz auf Blitz mit fürchterlichem Schein,
Der Donner rollte noch mit grasslichem Gebrülle.
Allein im Augenblick nahm eine sanfte Stille
Die fast betäubte Welt von neuem ein. . . .

The deistic impulse was directed toward nature; since the divine principle had revealed itself in nature, man venerated that principle by closely observing nature. But such close observation had secondary effects: it became, with continued practice, an end in itself. The notion of edification was lost. The Creator was inadvertently removed from creation; only now and then was a hasty nod of recollection sent in his direction. His presence remained, however, for a long time—as the guardian of morality.

Other factors contributed to a keener, broader, and deeper portrayal of the objective world. The bourgeoisie had grown into the position of the dominant class in England, and with its solid enterprises, its growing economic institutions and practices, its Protestant morality, it won a place for itself in the new narrative works. The great English novels, which began pouring out in rapid succession from the beginning of the eighteenth century on, no longer use the middle class merely as their setting. They are identified with the bourgeoisie, a self-assertive bourgeoisie which professes its own independently developed purposes and values. Hitherto—and in the French novel all the way down to Stendhal (with the sole exception of Rousseau)—the bourgeoisie had been merely the foil of the nobility. The mores of the nobility remained the standard for all classes. But Daniel Defoe's *Robinson Crusoe*, with which the new English novel began in 1719, opened with a statement of the middle-class credo. Indeed, the novel marked new departures in many respects. Young Crusoe is tempted by the lure of adventurous voyages into strange regions. His father warns him "that these things were either too far above me, or too far below me; that mine was the middle State, or what might be called the upper Station of *Low Life*, which he had found by long Experience was the best State in the World, the most suited to human Happiness, not exposed to the Miseries and Hardships, the Labour and Sufferings of the mechanick Part of Mankind, and not embarass'd with the Pride, Luxury, Ambition and Envy of the upper Part of Mankind. . . . *That* the middle Station of Life was calculated for all kinds of Virtues and all kinds of Enjoyments; that Peace and Plenty were the Hand-maids of a middle Fortune; that Temperance, Moderation, Quietness, Health, Society, all agreeable Diversions, and all desirable Pleasures, were the Blessings attending the middle Station of Life; that this Way Men went silently and smoothly thro' the World, and comfortably out of it, not embarrass'd with the Labours of the Hands or of the Head . . . not enrag'd with the Passion of Envy, or secret burning Lust of Ambition for great things; but in easy Circumstances . . . and sensibly tasting the Sweets of living. . . ."[15]

Middle-class business life and its interests brought the material constituents of reality into the foreground. Or rather, they began to isolate those constituents; scientific precision was concurrently having a similar effect in its field. Characteristic of this tendency was the separating of social and local description from the narrative context. John Gay's *Trivia, or the Art of Walking the Streets of London* (1716) is a detailed topographical description of the city in verse. It deals with incidents of daily life and the perils of the stroller. The verse form and the metaphorical allusions to the gods of classical antiquity are employed only with satiric intent, in contrast to Thomson's *The Seasons*. Defoe wrote extensive studies of social and meteorological disasters (*A Journal of the Plague Year, Some Account of the Great and Terrible Fire in*

---

[15] Text is from the fourth edition of 1719, pp. 3-4.

London in 1666, *The Storm*, etc.). Experiences and information gathered in the course of his manifold business projects find their way into his books or accumulate to make a separate book, such as the *Tour Through the Whole Island of Great Britain*, which is the summation of seventeen different journeys. Like his Colonel Jack in the novel of that name, Defoe was "always upon the Inquiry, asking Questions of things done in publick, as well as in private." It was characteristic of him, as well as of the whole era, that the businessman and the researcher were united in one person: "A true-bred Merchant is a universal Scholar." His facts were often quite unreliable, full of exaggerations and often enough intermixed with arbitrary fictions, where his experience fell short of what was needed. For example, in *Robinson Crusoe* he places penguins at the mouth of the Orinoco—he himself never saw the tropics. But his attitude, as a narrator, is that of a scientific empiricist, who tells his story by tracing the minute stages of the happenings. In Boccaccio, for example, the description of the plague is brief, taking only a few pages. Its purpose is merely to establish why the young people are fleeing the city and want to entertain one another by telling stories. Defoe's essay on the plague is an extensive memorandum, replete with "documentary" eye-witness accounts, ordinances, and statistics. Crusoe's shipwreck, which results in his being cast ashore on the island, and his arrangements there, could scarcely have been described more precisely and logically by an American naturalist writing in the twentieth century. What Defoe called "homely plain writing" was the first naturalistic language in the history of narrative.

Robinson Crusoe, moreover, is far more than the classic tale of travel and adventure that delighted the petty bourgeoisie of its time and still has the power to entertain our own youth. Granted, one can easily recognize in it the pattern of the picaresque novel which dominated the first centuries of the modern era, as well as the popular travel books of the day (Dampier, Knox, Woodes Rogers).[16] It was probably inspired by the story of Alexander Selkirk, the Scottish seaman who after a quarrel with his captain had himself landed on a South Seas island, where he lived for four and a half years, until he was picked up. But what distinguishes the novel from these models is its new burden of symbolic and parabolic meaning.

The story of Defoe's own life is recast into the destiny of Crusoe. Crusoe rejects the slow but sure progress of an ordinary middle-class career for adventurous voyages. But the pursuit of profit leads to nothing but shipwrecks

[16] The travel novel has a long history, starting with the *Odyssey*, Lucian, Apollonius of Tyre, and Oriental tales and going on to the forerunners of *Robinson Crusoe*. The first "Crusoe" was not Defoe's, but Henry Neville's in his *Isle of Pines* (1688), which anticipates many of the details found in *Crusoe*. Neville's story was promptly translated into German and inspired Grimmelshausen's Crusoesque flight in Book Six of *Simplicissimus*. In the travel tales of the prescientific age scarcely any boundary can be drawn between reportage and free fantasy. "The *Thousand and One Nights*," writes Gaston Maspero (*Les contes populaires de l'Egypte ancienne*, 9th edn. [Paris, 1911], p. lxxi), "are no more fantastic than the serious histories of the Moslem Middle Ages. Nor did the man of Cairo who wrote the seven voyages of Sinbad need to borrow his material from any earlier story; he had only to read his most serious writers or to listen to sailors and merchants who had returned from faraway places, to gather in abundance the stuff for his romances" ("Les *Mille et une nuits*, ne sont pas ici plus mensongères que les histories sérieuses du moyen âge musulman. Aussi bien le bourgeois du Caire qui écrivit les sept voyages de Sindbad n'avait-il pas besoin d'en emprunter les données à un conte antérieur: il n'avait qu'à lire les auteurs les plus graves ou qu'à écouter les matelots et les marchands revenus de loin, pour y recueillir à foison la matière de ses romans").

and distress. Defoe, similarly, undertook dangerous commercial enterprises and political risks that brought him to bankruptcies, prison, and the pillory. And Crusoe's physical loneliness on the island reflects the author's sense of spiritual solitude. It is remarkable that the symbolism of the story serves as the underpinning of its truthfulness, a truthfulness demanded both by the practical-minded middle-class public and Defoe's Puritan conscience. (The naturalistic exactitude, incidentally, is also meant to reinforce the credibility of the story; in turn, this requirement of truth or plausibility in the narrative provides a further impetus to exact observation.) "The Editor," Defoe declares in the preface to the first part, "believes the thing to be a just History of Fact; neither is there any Appearance of Fiction in it. . . ." He makes this still clearer in the preface to the third part, the *Serious Reflections of Robinson Crusoe* (1720), in which he says of himself: "Shipwreck'd often, tho' more by Land than by Sea . . . there's not a Circumstance in the imaginary Story, but has its just Allusion to a real Story. . . ." The following passage in the third part is further evidence of how urgent such self-reassurance was to him: "This supplying a Story by Invention, is certainly a most scandalous Crime . . . it is a sort of Lying that makes a great Hole in the Heart, at which by Degrees a Habit of Lying enters in. . . ."[17]

The didactic moralistic meaning of the novel cannot be separated from its personal meaning. The story of Crusoe is also a lesson in the ways of divine Providence.[18]

[17] Text is from the edition of 1720, p. 113.

[18] The preface states: "The Story is told with Modesty, with Seriousness, and with a religious Application of Events . . . to the Instruction of others by this Example, and to justify and honour the Wisdom of Providence in all the Variety of our Circumstances, let them happen how they will."

Repeatedly, Providence places before Crusoe the opportunity for well-regulated advancement. First he is offered the prosperity of his paternal home. Then his Brazilian plantation flourishes. Then again he manages his bare survival on the island and is at last rescued and returned to the middle-class order of things. In between these events come the intensifying warnings and punishments for his repeated flightiness and broken pledges: storms, slavery—from which he succeeds in escaping to Brazil—and then, when he is still not content and would rather throw up the slow growth of his plantation for the chance to get rich quick in the slave trade, the extreme peril of the shipwreck and his being cast ashore on the island. There, finally, after the idyll of a secure life with his animal family, come the terrifying visits of the cannibals, which result in his acquiring his human companion, Friday. Throughout, divine guidance seems to be at work; and that element is still detectable in the book's third level of meaning. For the story also provides his audience, newly awakened to thinking about economic life, with a contemporary paradigm of the fundamentals of economics. Crusoe is shown inventing, or rather reinventing by sheer reason under the goad of necessity, certain elementary tools and aids such as the shovel, the spade, the wheel, the ladder, and so on. Then comes the taming of animals and the planting of grain. Defoe derives the lesson that by the proper use of reason anyone can become the master of every mechanical skill. "I made abundance of Things, even without Tools, and some with no more Tools than an Adze and a Hatchet, which perhaps were never made that way before, and that with infinite Labour . . ." (p. 79).

On the other hand, his condition reveals to Crusoe the relative value or worthlessness of all goods, and the full use-value of everything man really needs when he has nothing but what he needs: "But all I could make use of, was, All that was valuable. I had enough to eat, and to supply my Wants, and what was all the rest to me? . . . I had . . . a Parcel of Money, as well Gold as Silver, about thirty six Pounds Sterling: Alas! there the nasty sorry useless Stuff lay! I had no manner of Business for it; and I often thought with myself, that I would . . . have given it all for Six pennyworth of *Turnip* and *Carrot* Seed out of *England*, or for a Handful of *Pease* and *Beans*, and a Bottle of Ink . . ." (pp. 152-153).

The moral and religious vacillations in Crusoe's—and Defoe's—career reflect the secularizing shift in Calvinism, which was taking place at this very time. Calvinism had originally started from the static position of Wyclif and Luther, who taught that it was every man's duty to serve God by remaining at his post in the calling in which God had placed him. Calvinism was more activistically disposed than Lutheranism only by its tendency to include vocational life, and secular life in general, more directly and obligatorily within the sphere of religious justification.[19] But under the pressure of economic developments—overseas trade, finance, manufacturing—Calvinism grew increasingly more dynamic and worldly. Ultimately, it came to shift religious justification more and more into economic pursuits and monetary success. A man's calling ceased to be God-given as such. Rather, what were God-given were his talents, his capacity for making rational choices and engaging in undertakings.[20]

---

[19] ". . . at the day of Doom, men shall be judged according to their fruits. It will not be said then, *Did you believe?* but, Were you *Doers*, or *Talkers* only?" (Bunyan, *The Pilgrim's Progress* [London, 1678], Facsimile Text Society Edition [New York, 1928], p. 109).

[20] "God hath given to man reason for this use, that he should first consider, then choose, then put in execution; and it is a

Success was the proof of God's grace. In Richard Baxter's *Christian Directory* (1678) we are told: "Be wholly taken up in diligent business of your lawful callings, when you are not exercised in the more immediate service of God." But in the same tract the next step was already taken: "If God show you a way in which you may lawfully get more than in another way (without wrong to your soul or to any other), if you refuse this and choose the less gainful way, you cross one of the ends of your Calling and you refuse to be God's steward."[21] The complex of problems faced by Crusoe—and Defoe—moves between these two poles.

Women are completely absent from the story of Robinson Crusoe. Defoe followed up that novel with two counterpoises, *Moll Flanders* (1722) and *Lady Roxana* (1724), in which he more than made up for the lack of erotic incident in the earlier work. The implication is that a man's adventures take place in business enterprises, while a woman's take place in her love life. The male adventurer sins actively by overstepping the bounds divine Providence has set for him. The female adventuress sins passively in that under the pressure of circumstances, and ensnared by temptation, she abandons human moderation in love and social moderation in marriage, and becomes a whore. The confessions of both women deal with the gradual slide from virtue to vice; the stories are told to point a moral and both conclude on a note of repentance. But the didactic intention is no

---

preposterous and brutish thing to fix or fall upon any weighty business, such as a calling or condition of life, without a careful pondering it in the balance of sound reason" (Richard Steele, *The Tradesman's Calling* [London, 1648], quoted in R. H. Tawney, *Religion and the Rise of Capitalism* [New York, 1926], Chap. IV, p. 241).

[21] Quoted in Tawney, p. 242.

longer central to the tale, as it was in *Robinson Crusoe.*
Rather, it is only tacked on in order to justify the relatively lascivious material. What distinguishes the stories
of these Protestant adventuresses from Grimmelshausen's
Mother Courage or Chaucer's Wife of Bath is the puritanical guilty conscience, which panders to its own shame
by dwelling on the cruder details. The presentation is
shallower and vaguer than in *Robinson Crusoe.* The detailed observation and intimacy with the subject that
marked Defoe's travel novel and social descriptions are
somewhat lacking in these later works; the author lapses
into a bare and slapdash account of events. The characterization of individuals is less specific. The one thing
Defoe successfully draws with a firm, sensitive line is the
gradual disappearance of moral inhibitions in these
women.[22]

[22] The following passage from *Roxana* is typical of the attitude of these transitional novels: the curious interweaving of
standard bourgeois morality with covert bourgeois prurience.
Morality has taken the place of humanly sensitive dignity; rules
and scruples substitute for the discipline of natural feeling. It
becomes apparent that institutionalized "propriety" is not only
a screen for actual lasciviousness, but even serves to inflame it.
The result is a new and typically bourgeois problem. Roxana's
ne'er-do-well, unloved husband has deserted her, leaving her in
misery with her four children. Relatives have rescued the children; she herself is courted by a wealthy businessman whose
gifts and kindness she at first accepts honorably, until at last she
yields to him out of gratitude. They move to Paris where they
live together as man and wife—she cannot marry him because
her husband is still alive, his whereabouts unknown. Although
she lives in an orderly household, enjoys general esteem, and
loves her present companion (later, when he dies, she records,
"I almost cried myself to death for him . . . indeed I loved him
to a degree inexpressible"), she already feels in her present unmarried situation that she is the fallen woman she eventually
becomes. In the scene below we perceive something of the real
character of the middle-class Protestant. It takes place between

In Daniel Defoe, then, a variety of fresh motives conjoin to make the narrator observe matters which had previously been left in darkness. These motives are: the now-dominant bourgeoisie's attentiveness to material things; scientific empiricism; overseas explorations with their ac-

---

Roxana and her devoted servant Amy, who, coming from a less "respectable" class, is blessed from the start by fewer moral scruples than her mistress. She has, however, more human delicacy and manages to keep that quality through thick and thin:

Amy was dressing me one morning, for now I had two maids, and Amy was my chambermaid. "Dear madame," says Amy, "what! a'nt you with child yet?" "No, Amy," says I; "nor any sign of it."

"Law, madam!" says Amy, "what have you been doing? Why, you have been married a year and a half. I warrant your master would have got me with child twice in that time." "It may be so, Amy," says I. "Let him try, can't you?" "No," says Amy; "you'll forbid it now. Before, I told you he should, with all my heart; but I won't now, now he's all your own." "Oh," says I, "Amy, I'll freely give you my consent. It will be nothing at all to me. Nay, I'll put you to bed to him myself one night or other, if you are willing." "No, madam, no," says Amy, "not now he's yours." . . .

After supper that night, and before we were risen from table, I say to him [her husband], Amy being by, "Hark ye, Mr ——, do you know that you are to lie with Amy to-night?" "No, not I," says he; but turns to Amy, "Is it so, Amy?" says he. "No, sir," says she. "Nay, don't say no, you fool; did not I promise to put you to bed to him?" But the girl said "No" still and it passed off.

At night, when we came to go to bed, Amy came into the chamber to undress me, and her master slipped into bed first; then I began, and told him all that Amy had said about my not being with child, and of her being with child twice in that time. "Ay, Mrs Amy," says he, "I believe so too. Come hither, and we'll try." But Amy did not go. "Go, you fool," says I, "can't you? I freely give you both leave." But Amy would not go . . . I sat her down, pulled off her stock-

companying emphasis on description; the middle-class hunger for "true history," in the light of which the narrator must strive harder to achieve credibility; and finally, Puritan moral scruples.

---

ings and shoes, and all her clothes piece by piece, and led her to the bed to him. . . . She pulled back a little, would not let me pull off her clothes at first, but it was hot weather, and she had not many clothes on . . . and at last, when she saw I was in earnest, she let me do what I would. So I fairly stripped her, and then I threw open the bed and thrust her in. . . .

Amy, I dare say, began now to repent, and would fain have got out of bed again; but he said to her, "Nay, Amy, you see your mistress has put you to bed; 'tis all her doing; you must blame her." So he held her fast, and the wench being naked in the bed with him, it was too late to look back, so she lay still and let him do what he would with her.

Had I looked upon myself as a wife, you cannot suppose I would have been willing to have let my husband lie with my maid, much less before my face, for I stood by all the while; but as I thought myself a whore, I cannot say, but that it was something designed in my thoughts that my maid should be a whore, too, and should not reproach me with it.

Amy, however, less vicious than I, was grievously out of sorts the next morning . . . and there was no pacifying her; she was a whore, a slut, and she was undone! undone! and cried almost all day.

The husband, too, took the matter amiss afterwards, blaming not Roxana but the victim, Amy: "he hated her heartily, and could, I believe, have killed her after it, and he told me so, for he thought this a vile action . . ." (*The Fortunate Mistress or a History of the Life of Lady Roxana*, in Defoe, *Romances and Narratives*, ed. George A. Aitken [London, 1899], XII, 48-50). Roxana herself continues to have pangs of conscience, not because of this monstrous act of hers—for later on she again induces her husband to sleep with Amy—but on account of the "sin" of being unwed. Yet she would have looked upon the matter differently if only she could have gone to confession and

But there were other and still more powerful influences which sprang from developing science. For science
was changing the very character of the reality which was
the storyteller's subject. The discoveries of Tycho Brahe,
Kepler, Galileo, and Newton extended the known world,
and therefore worldliness, into new cosmic realms. Entirely new realms now became susceptible to analytic
treatment. Such regions had previously lain outside the
range of the senses and had therefore represented a supernatural, extrahuman, mythic reality, a reality with which
only a magical relation was possible. But now these same
regions had been moved entirely within the sphere of
human empiricism. In expanding man's real world these
developments had also begun to pervade that world tech-
nically, instrumentally, in other words, with materialized
abstractions. But in addition—and this is what primarily
concerns us here—the conception of the universe that
resulted from these conquests introduced a new pictorial
quality into art, a new conscious coherence and richness
of interrelationships which begins to be seen in the works
of the eighteenth century and is fully present in the literature of the Romantic period.

This movement had its start in the astronomy and natural philosophy of the fifteenth and sixteenth centuries·
Tycho Brahe's discovery of a hitherto unnoticed, un-
usually brilliant star in Cassiopeia (1572) and Kepler's
addition of another such star in 1604 shattered the Aris-
totelian conception of a stable, finite firmament populated by a fixed and known number of immutable heav-

---

obtained absolution, "but though I was a whore, yet I was a
Protestant whore, and could not act as if I was popish." The
crudest eroticism in Lucian, Apuleius, Aretino, or Rétif de la
Bretonne strikes one as pure compared to such excesses of puritanical morality, whose heat is merely magnified by the formal
pangs of conscience.

enly bodies. For not only was "Tycho's star" new; it was
more than that. It was, as Galileo declared it to be in the
year of its discovery; a "nova," that is, a star which suddenly displays an extraordinarily powerful burst of light
for a few hours or days, and just as swiftly sinks back
into inconspicuousness. In 1608 came the construction of
the telescope (in Holland, England, and Italy).[23] Galileo
improved the instrument and discovered four unknown
satellites of Jupiter and a countless quantity of new stars.
What is more, he was able to recognize the hitherto mys-
terious Milky Way as a gigantic mass of stars. The new
instrument also called into question the time-honored
image of the moon. For centuries poets had extolled the
gentle, untroubled sheen of this "glowing sphere." It
now turned out that the moon possessed not "a smooth,
shiny but a rough and uneven surface, and like the face
of the earth is everywhere full of mighty excrescences,
deep abysses and convolutions." Galileo reported all
these discoveries in his *Sidereus nuncius*, published in
1610, which had a tremendous, revolutionizing impact
on men's minds throughout Europe.

The vast and crucial change in man's view of the cosmos brought about by such astronomical discoveries
spelled the end of the closed world system. There was
instead a recognition of the infinitude of the universe.
Earlier, in 1530, Copernicus had shifted the cosmic center from the earth to the sun. He had shown that the
earth was in motion, moving around the sun; and thus he
had enlarged the conception of the solar system's size
and distances.

Earlier still, moreover, a kind of mathematical mysticism had sprung up in the philosophy of the transitional
period, a marriage of mystical pantheism (Meister Eck-

[23] The telescope was actually invented by Roger Bacon in
the thirteenth century.

hart) with mathematical ideas. Nicholas of Cues (1401-1464), whose doctrines contained the seeds of later theism and Deism, as well as of modern cosmological quantification, developed his conception of the microcosm from the mathematical notion of the infinitesimally small: the point. His microcosm is a concentrated mirror image ("specula contractiora") of the infinitely large, which is to say, God's absolute infinity, and of the macrocosm, which is the "contracted" infinity of the universe in space and time. God is simultanteously the infinitely large and the infinitely small, "coincidentia maximi cum minimo." To Nicholas, only God was truly infinite and as such was not only the ground, center, and purpose of the universe, but also its infinite circumference. His disciple Giordano Bruno (1548?-1600), in his dialogue *Dell' infinito universo e dei mondi* (1584), dared to assert the infinity of the universe itself even before astronomical investigation had suggested such a possibility. (In order to propagate his doctrines, Bruno traveled throughout Europe, also visiting England.) In his treatise *De triplice minimo* he discussed the threefold form of the infinitesimally small: mathematically as a point, physically as an atom, metaphysically as a monad, the individual entity.

This "minimum" previsioned by natural philosophy was empirically revealed at about the same time by the invention of the microscope, again in Holland and Italy. The development of this instrument took place more gradually and less sensationally than that of the telescope. The public did not become really aware of it until later on (actually, after 1663); then, however, it exerted a much broader popular influence than the telescope. As a consequence of Robert Hooke's experiments and especially after Anton van Leeuwenhoek's investigations with a greatly improved instrument (from 1674 on), observations with the microscope became a fashionable pastime in English society. Amateur experimenters of both sexes ("virtuosos" and "virtuosas") became curiosity collectors and went about with pocket microscopes as some people do today with Geiger counters, looking for Leeuwenhoek's "animalcules" in whatever came their way. They found tiny "water flyes" and "water lice," "eels" and "worms" in blood and saliva. They admired the perfection and variety of these miniature organic structures, which they regarded as representing the "secret world" of nature or God. All substances and indeed the whole atmosphere seemed to be populated by tiny organisms, like a farcical confirmation of the ubiquitously animate universe that Nicholas of Cues and Giordano Bruno had postulated. English literature of the period reacted at first to the popularity of the microscope with satires upon this fad.[24] "Whatever appears trivial and obscene in the common notions of the world," commented the *Tatler* of 20 August 1710, "looks grave and philosophical in the eyes of a virtuoso."

Thus man suddenly beheld himself placed between two natural infinities, or rather, between two forms of the same natural infinity. With his new instrumental organs of perception he looked into spheres hitherto unreachable, and blocked out ever broader areas for investigation. Along with this accomplishment came a new sense of metaphysical insecurity, a profound terror at the collapse of the well-proportioned and immutable cosmic order. John Donne, who had at first lightheartedly mocked the new astronomy in his dialogue *Ignatius*, sud-

[24] Cf. Marjorie Nicolson, *Science and Imagination* (Ithaca, N.Y., 1956), p. iv, and pp. 155-234: "The Microscope and English Imagination."

denly became prophetically aware, in 1610, of its enormously serious implications, of the "disproportion," "rude incongruitie," and "mutability" of the universe:

> . . . in these Constellations then arise
> New starres, and old doe vanish from our eyes:
> As though heav'n suffered earthquakes, peace or war,
> When new Towers rise, and old demolish'd are.[25]

> And new Philosophy calls all in doubt,

> . . . .

> And freely men confesse that this world's spent,
> When in the Planets, and the Firmament
> They seek so many new; they see that this
> Is crumbled out againe to his Atomies.
> 'Tis all in peeces, all cohaerence gone;
> All just supply, and all Relation. . . .[26]

From these contemplations Donne all at once arrives at a realization of our whole modern quandary: that man has embraced the vast dimensions of the universe and simultaneously impoverished the human person.

> Man hath weav'd out a net, and this net throwne
> Upon the Heavens, and now they are his owne.
> Loth to goe up the hill, or labour thus
> To goe to heaven, we make heaven come to us.[27]

And on the other hand:

> This man, whom God did wooe . . .

> . . . .

> This man, so great that all that is, is his,
> Oh what a trifle, and poore thing he is!
> If man were anything, he's nothing now.[28]

[25] "An Anatomie of the World. The First Anniversary," ll. 259-262, in *The Poems of John Donne*, ed. H.J.C. Grierson (Oxford, 1912).
[26] "The First Anniversary," ll. 205, 209-214.
[27] "The First Anniversary," ll. 279-282.
[28] "The First Anniversary," ll. 167, 169-171.

The destruction of the equilibrium and stability of the universe was troubling enough. But almost more disturbing was the uncertainty regarding what new researches might reveal. Men began to conjecture many unknown worlds and creatures, a possible plurality of worlds. Bruno had already considered it ridiculous "to think like the common rabble that there are no other creatures, no other intelligence and reason than those known to us," and "that there are no more planets than those we have hitherto known." By the time of Fontenelle's *Entretiens sur la pluralité des mondes* (1686) this view had become established. It stimulated the Enlightenment; it also stimulated literary fantasies, for the most part satiric, about strange worlds and creatures.

The many allusions and explicit references to the new instruments and new cosmological findings in the prose and satiric verse of the seventeenth and eighteenth centuries are still only superficial phenomena. Even the new metaphors and phrases, which here and there reflected scientific experience, did not yet affect the mode of artistic vision. But we can see the transformation of the whole way of looking at the world—first brought about by the telescope—by comparing Milton's *Paradise Lost* with Dante's *Divina Commedia*.

Both are Christian epics proposing to set forth the sovereignty of God and the sacrifice of Christ. But the Catholic epic is static, the Protestant epic dynamic and dramatic. The *Divina Commedia* takes the form of a pilgrimage by the poet through the universes. It is essentially a topography—*topographie raisonée et imagée*—of the dogmatic cosmos into which pagan, Judaic, and Christian history are incorporated symbolically and allegorically (or rather, symbo-allegorically, for at this transitional juncture symbol and allegory coincide). By the fiat of God, these different strands of history are reconciled. At the center is man's situation: man is caught between the various hells and heavens. At the same time God has imposed upon him free will. The narrative traces his manifold missteps and delinquencies, and his exaltation by redemption.

Paradise Lost is essentially history, but not human history. Man is still confined within prehistory. Milton concerns himself with the preterrestrial history of the struggle between cosmic forces which determine man's providential fate; man himself is only the object and the theater of war. In this respect Milton's epic represents a prelude to *Faust*. The protagonist and primal sinner is not man himself, but the rebellious angel Satan, who tries to snatch man from God. In Dante the rebellion of the angels is a closed chapter; Lucifer has been hurled down from heaven and by his fall has created the abysmal crater of hell, at whose bottom he is held fast. Milton's Satan is a roving warlord actually engaged in his revolutionary operations.

The poet Dante is identical with his subject, the man who passes through the theater of his own inner and outer experiences toward the goal of salvation. The poet Milton has divided aims. His conscious purpose is glorification of the Lord. But as is well known, and all too easily sensed, his heart is on the side of Satan, the hero of freedom. Milton's man is contained not within the Adam who is merely a victim of the cosmic civil war, but in the Satan who exuberantly asserts his total selfhood. His is a real, totally independent, even libertine freedom of the will, not a freedom hypocritically controlled by God:

> . . . Hail, horrors, hail
> Infernal world, and thou profoundest Hell
> Receive thy new Possessor: One who brings

A mind not to be chang'd by Place or Time.
The mind is its own place, and in itself
Can make a Heav'n of Hell, a Hell of Heav'n.
What matter where, if I be still the same?

. . . .

. . . Here at least
We shall be free; th' Almighty hath not built
Here for his envy, will not drive us hence!
Here we may reign secure, and in my choyce
To reign is worth ambition, though in Hell:
Better to reign in Hell, than serve in Heav'n.[29]

Here, beneath the Puritan disguise, man's real autonomy already emerges. It is an altogether unfettered self-determination that goes far beyond the freedom of choice imposed by God.

For Dante, hell was a dominion of God, a many-leveled and subdivided Hades beyond the beyond, in which human sinners languished and did penance. In *Paradise Lost* the first hell encountered is that of the expelled angels. But Milton's real hell is not this infernal realm itself, not the residence of Satan, that Pandaemonium where he holds a council of war with his peers, not the place where many of the fallen angels, in a quiet valley, sing of their own heroic destiny:

With notes Angelical to many a Harp
Their own Heroic deeds and hapless fall
By doom of Battel; and complain that Fate
Free Vertue should enthrall to Force or Chance.[30]

Once again, this time by the sweetness of the song—for after all, they are angels—infernality is checked:

[29] *Paradise Lost*, Book I, ll. 250-256, 258-263, in *The Complete Poetical Works of John Milton*, ed. Rev. H. C. Beeching (London, 1911).
[30] Book II, ll. 548-551.

Their song was partial, but the harmony
(What could it less when Spirits immortal sing?)
Suspended Hell. . . .[31]

This part of hell becomes almost a colony of paradise,
as does that hill where others "in thoughts more elevate"
discuss questions of Providence, of free will and of fate,
questions which "with a pleasing sorcerie could charm /
Pain for a while or anguish."[32] The real hell, in fact, is
not even that inhospitable region where roam the more
enterprising members of Satan's following "in Squadrons
and gross Bands," seeking a better climate for settlement
or attempting to reach the river Lethe, which bestows
forgetfulness. Milton's true hell begins beyond the bor-
ders of hell, in that tremendous cosmic no-man's-land
between hell and heaven where Chaos reigns. Indeed it
embraces them both. It is beyond the Lethe where

. . . a frozen Continent
Lies dark and wilde, beat with perpetual storms
Of Whirlwind and dire Hail, which on firm land
Thaws not, but gathers heap . . .

. . . .

A gulf profound . . .

. . . .

. . . the parching Air
Burns frore, and cold performs th' effect of fire.[33]

And beyond the gates of hell, which Sin and Death
throw open to Satan for his journey of exploration
through the spheres:

Before their eyes in sudden view appear
The secrets of the hoarie deep, a dark
Illimitable Ocean without bound,

[31] Book II, ll. 552-554.   [32] Book II, ll. 566-567.
[33] Book II, ll. 587-590, 592, 594-595.

Without dimension, where length, breadth and highth,
And time and place are lost; where eldest Night
And *Chaos*, Ancestors of Nature, hold
Eternal *Anarchie*, amidst the noise
Of endless warrs, and by confusion stand.
For hot, cold, moist and dry, four Champions fierce
Strive here for Maistrie, and to Battel bring
Their embryon Atoms. . . .

. . . .

. . . Into this wilde Abyss,
The Womb of nature and perhaps her Grave . . .

. . . .

Into this wild Abyss the warie fiend
Stood on the brink of Hell and look'd a while,
Pondering his Voyage. . . .[34]

From above, Christ with his angels regards the same
scene before he begins his journey of creation at God's
command:

On heav'nly ground they stood and from the shore
They view'd the vast immeasurable Abyss
Outrageous as a Sea, dark, wasteful, wilde,
Up from the bottom turn'd by furious windes
And surging waves, as Mountains to assault
Heav'ns highth, and with the Center mix the Pole.[35]

Both God and Satan look down as through a telescope,
and in one comprehensive glance take in the whole
world.

The new conception of cosmic depth entangled Milton in insoluble contradictions with his theology, but he
did not dare to relinquish the latter. Although he was
overwhelmed by the conception of the "vast, immeasurable Abyss" surrounding the two residences of God

[34] Book II, ll. 890-900, 910-911, 917-919.
[35] Book VII, ll. 210-215.

and the devil, and although the world created by God is wrested from empty and formless infinity, God tells his Son:

> ... ride forth and bid the Deep
> Within appointed bounds be Heav'n and Earth,
> Boundless the Deep, because I Am who fill
> Infinitude, nor vacuous the space.[36]

Although the number of the stars is immeasurable and the number of worlds, inhabited or uninhabited, uncertain, God himself is infinite and omnipotent, creative and puritanically strict, filling all of space and yet withdrawn into himself:

> Though I uncircumscrib'd my self retire
> And put not forth my goodness, which is free
> To act or not, Necessitie and Chance
> Approach not mee, and what I will is Fate.[37]

Compared to Dante's great and integral poem, this wide-ranging epic was inherently contradictory and uncontrolled, a transitional opus expressing the rift that had developed between science and Biblical orthodoxy. But the new reach and openness of the universe entered into its picture of the cosmos, the sense of infinity which the telescope had introduced. The closed cosmos had been breached; and now there arose a host of questions and conflicts with which pure science could not concern itself.

Dante's universe had been a well-ordered, finite world held within the infinite will of the Creator. The planets and the stars of the firmament were enclosed and moved by the *primum mobile*, and above in the empyrean sat enthroned the all-embracing ruler of the universe.[38]

---

[36] Book VII, ll. 166-169. [37] Book VII, ll. 170-173.
[38] "E questo cielo non ha altro dove / che la mente divina, in

Man's relation to the universe was identical with his relation to God. Milton adds a further dimension to this realm, splitting it and making it undergo a twofold transposition: beyond the beyond, beyond the Elysian and the infernal regions, true cosmic space opens out for the first time. His questioning involves not only the relationship of man to God but also the relationship of God himself to the cosmos. Adamite man remains caught up in Puritan providentiality. But the man lying hidden within Satan has liberated himself totally from divine rule and stands shuddering on the brink of the transdivine depths of the universe. In Dante, man is at the center (egocentrically, as it were), but dependent on a divine cosmic order. In Milton, man as such is no longer at the crux of the drama; but in his satanic autonomy he stands in an infinitely expanded, profane universe. Consciousness has conquered new realms.

The new instruments and the discoveries they made possible expanded poetic vision in other directions also, by the wider scope they gave to analysis. Newtonian optics conferred upon light a new significance as the creator of color. The spectrum, the rainbow, unfolded its dynamic, iridescent splendor, reanimating the purely geometrical structure of the Galilean and Cartesian world of objects. The "philosophical eye" delighted in the new, vibrant, interacting coloration of sunrises and sunsets, in the varying hues of daylight, in clouds, hunting dogs, butterfly wings.[39]

---

che s'accende / l'amor che 'l volge e la virtú ch'ei piove" (*Par.* XXVII, 109-111).

[39] One example will serve for many: "Spread on each wing the florid seasons glow, / Shaded and verg'd with the celestial bow, / Where colours blend an ever varying dye / And wanton in their gay exchanges vie" (Henry Brooke, *Universal Beauty,*

In contrast to the revelations of the telescope, which literature on the whole greeted with unequivocal enthusiasm, the new world opened up by the microscope was received with extremely mixed emotions. The fad for amateur anatomical and literary investigations made the microscope an object of literary ridicule.[40] The notion of ubiquitous swarms of living things, "the living cloud of Pestilence," revealed by the microscope, stirred horror and revulsion in Thomson. He considered it one of the mercies of creation that all the "worlds in worlds enclosed" remain concealed from man's unaided eye. Other poets, for example Pope, asked why man had not been created originally with a microscopic eye. At any rate, this instrument also had an impact on all of European writing, and particularly Italian and English literature, in the seventeenth and eighteenth centuries. Nevertheless, the microscope did not at first exert an influence upon poetic vision and the poets' creative faculty comparable to the effect of the telescope upon Milton. Such deeper influence can be observed only in the case of Swift.

Along with the factors which both expanded and concentrated the field of vision and thus the field of consciousness, we must reckon with the satiric spirit so prevalent in English literature. We have already seen, in connection with the epic writers of the Renaissance and baroque periods, the extent to which satire sharpens observation. In this age of a rising middle class and ecclesiastical conflicts, socially critical satire was the dominant

---

Book V, ll. 278-281). See also Marjorie Nicolson, *Newton Demands the Muse* (Princeton, 1946), pp. 20ff.

[40] A wealth of examples are collected in Marjorie Nicolson's *Science and Imagination*, pp. 155ff. The most amusing is the description of the dissection of "The Beau's Head" and "The Coquette's Heart."

literary tendency in England. The great "wits" of the age excelled in it—Samuel Butler, Dryden, Pope, Arbuthnot, John Gay, Wycherley, Congreve, Richard Steele (not to be confused with the theologian of the same name), and, to a lesser degree, Defoe also. These satirists employed all the traditional forms, lyric, verse epic, novel, drama. In many, and some very prominent, cases, literary work actually took the form of pamphlet or diatribe. Circles like the Scriblerus Club, magazines like the *Spectator* and the *Tatler*, and the many popular coffee houses served as forums for often venomous debates and feuds—unlike France, where aristocratic salons served the same function. The satiric imagination was inclined to personify itself in such mythical figures as John Bull, Martinus Scriblerus, and Isaac Bickerstaff. Outshining all the lesser lights stands the great figure of Jonathan Swift, whose entire lifework consisted of caustic criticism. But the point is that he criticized not only contemporary social, political, and cultural conditions, but in them and beyond them the makeup of man himself.

In John Gay and Alexander Pope we can observe satire accomplishing the dissolution of mythological allegory. Their deities, nature spirits, and abstract personifications cease to be employed as anything but instruments of parody, ironic travesties, types, keys to social conditions. This is what gives works like Gay's *Trivia*, Pope's *Rape of the Lock* and *Dunciad*, Swift's *Battle of the Books* their peculiarly epicene character, their novel mixture of mythic heroics and soberly naturalistic fixation upon the object. In these writers we no longer have the naïve, uncontrolled confusion of materials and stylistic elements that we find in Rabelais and Grimmelshausen. Rather, the contrasts are deliberately employed as stylistic devices; they serve the purposes of persiflage just as much as the allegory does.

Pope's brilliant talent is impelled by personal spite and rancor, and often does not go beyond these emotions— "as Hags hold Sabbaths, less for joy than spite." The *Dunciad*, that aggressive squib on stupidity, is peculiarly airless; its linguistic wit, excited by and aimed at specific figures in society, is constantly overflowing and leaving no room to breathe. For all its extraordinary rhetorical acrobatics, and in spite of some magnificent passages in which the writer's long-accumulated bitterness and concomitant knowledge of humanity is grievously vented, it remains at bottom literary gossip. Swift, too, had a sharp eye for human weakness, and the linguistic agility that goes with it; but he was able to go beyond mere wordplay and pour his emotions of rage and contempt into a universal satire such as *Gulliver's Travels*.

The result is something without precedent or equal. In Swift the widest variety of traditions and tendencies converge. What is more important, they are forged into a unitary conception, integrated within a dominating consciousness. This integration is achieved by a consistently ironic exaggeration of human limits. The result is a coherence, a network of relationships among various realms which will be met with once again in Laurence Sterne and which prepares the way for the comprehensive consciousness of the Romantic movement, especially the German Romantic movement.

We have here a line of development in which *Gulliver's Travels* is enormously important. To grasp its full significance we must look back to an earlier stage, in fact to the starting point of the line: Rabelais' *Gargantua* and *Pantagruel*. In Rabelais' baroque work, and to a certain extent in Grimmelshausen's *Simplicissimus* as well, we will find a similar convergence of the most variegated elements, legendary, mythical, fabulous, historical, topical, and even scientific. We find references to and parodies of the explorations and travel narratives of the period, especially Alain Cartier's. In fact, the route of Pantagruel's travels in the fourth and fifth books probably follows the plan that so captivated man's mind at the time, the idea of reaching Cathay (China) by the Northwest Passage. We find the ancient tradition of utopia. Gargantua rules in Sir Thomas More's Utopia, the land of the Amaurotians, the "dark," "uncertain" people. Pantagruel on his sea voyage touches upon wildly fantastic islands, such as the island of the Macreons, the long-lived heroes and demons; the island of the hypocrites; the island of the wild chitterlings; of the Papefiges (antipapists) and Papemanes (Baptists); of Entelechy and Quintessence; of the birds; and of all kinds of monsters imaginable. But the Abbey of Theleme (the abbey of free will and agreeableness, *thélema*), that humanistic ideal of a community in which everyone may live as he pleases, is a utopia. The heroes are giants out of the fairy tales and chapbooks, who have, however, a taste for humanistic studies. Rabelais would have us turn away from the old scholastic book-knowledge and seek instead *la leçon des choses*. Thus Grandgousier sends his son Gargantua, and the latter his son Pantagruel in turn, to learn such empirical lessons. But quite apart from this message, the entire work is animated by an immense sportiveness, a sheer delight in satire.

Satire, in fact, has run wild in the work of Rabelais. Satire has become a passion permeating all of life. It is not a pose, not a general mood, and it is free of bitterness. It springs from the intensity of experience, from pleasure in effervescent expressiveness, from vivid exaggeration; indeed, exaggeration is the keynote of the whole narrative. The satire is carried along by this delight in exaggeration, propelled by it to fresh imaginative excesses, to an unflagging succession of monstrous fantasies and obscenities, to a Boschlike tumult of verbal and figurative creations and hybridizations. Everything is spawned by the moment, the product of careless and happy spontaneity—which is what gives the obscenity its robust magnificence. And yet, for all its wit, its intellectual deftness and sophistry, this gloriously hybrid creation remains naïve, a simple mélange of elements without inner consistency. The utopias, even the lovely human utopia of the Abbey of Theleme, are totally unpragmatic. The giants stride directly out of the chapbooks, and aside from representing humorously exaggerated vital forces they have no deeper meaning. The new empiricism of humanism is still prescientific, and thus mere theory. Disparate elements have not yet been shaped into a coherent conception.

If we consider Swift's *Gulliver* (published in 1726) against the background of *Gargantua*, we see at once that *Gulliver* is necessarily thinner in terms of sheer vitality, but artistically superior. The relationship among the varied elements is no longer a matter of mere mixture. Rather, there is an inner, an internalized, interpenetration and concentration. A ruling motif links all the stories, holding the elements together. That motif is the expansion of human limitations in all dimensions. By expanding man's physical and moral limits, and even the limits of longevity, Swift shows what these limits are, shows man's condition. The expansion takes place both in the negative and positive senses, that is to say, in satire and in utopianism. Granted, a trace of this can be found in certain passages of More's *Utopia*: but in that work, even more than in Rabelais, the satire remains a casual, superficial peppering. Moreover, it is not real satire, but rather humorous allusion to actual conditions. In *Gulliver* the satire is omnipresent. From the very start it is interwoven in many different ways with the utopian stories, until at the end the ultimate seriousness of the whole work emerges and satire is seen as part and parcel of the utopian idea itself.

A clear artistic intention permeates this work from beginning to end. Parody of the travel narrative, of the "true relation," such as Lucian had long ago undertaken, is still the guiding element in Rabelais' work. But this kind of parody is wholly incidental in *Gulliver's Travels*. The theme is sounded at the beginning, outside the book itself, in Gulliver's letter to his cousin-publisher; in the "publisher's" preface to the readers;[41] and once more at the end of the book. As a background element, it can be sensed all along in the practical and technical tone, the sly understatement of the adventurous tales. But it is not the real concern of the book—even less so than in *Robinson Crusoe*. And what was a principal concern of Pope's—a veiled portrayal of specific persons and contemporary events—is likewise incidental in Swift. Rather, the book deliberately progresses, part by part, from mere caustic social criticism to a ridiculing of scientific and spiritual attitudes and on to the blasphemously

[41] "The only Fault I find is, that the Author, after the Manner of Travellers, is a little too Circumstantial. There is an Air of Truth apparent through the Whole; and indeed, the Author was so distinguished for his Veracity, that it became a sort of Proverb among his Neighbours at *Redriff*, when any one affirm'd a Thing, to say, it was as true as if Mr. *Gulliver* had spoke it. . . . This Volume would have been at least twice as long, if I had not made bold to strike out innumerable Passages relating to the Winds and Tides . . . together with the minute Descriptions of the Management of the Ship in Storms, in the Style of Sailors: Likewise the Account of the Longitudes and Latitudes. . . ." (The text is that of the facsimile of the first edition, ed. Harold Williams [London, 1926].)

embittered condemnation of the human race as such. That condemnation strikes home with uncanny force precisely because it is couched as a travesty of a fable. In the account of the Lilliputians, utopia and satire are interlaced but remain independent of one another. The third chapter describes the original customs and laws of the people, which suggest a utopian state of ideal excellence. But what Gulliver actually finds is degeneration from the original state; he encounters corruption and servility, follies and intrigues. Swift's burlesque parables reflect actual English and European conditions. For example, rope-dancing for the amusement of the ruler "is only practised by those Persons who are Candidates for great Employments, and high Favour, at Court."[42] Distinctions are awarded to those who demonstrate agility in "leaping and creeping." Paralleling the folly of human factionalism and wars, there is the fanatical struggle between the Small-Endians and the Big-Endians, those who hold that eggs should be broken at the small end and those who favor the big end. The exiled Big-Endians find refuge and support in the neighboring kingdom of Blefuscu, and bloody wars flare up over this question, with both sides arguing their cause by citations from their common sacred scriptures.[43] Gulliver learns by ex-

[42] Part I, Chap. III.

[43] "The books of the Big-Endians have been long forbidden, and the whole Party rendred incapable by Law of holding Employments. During the Course of these Troubles, the Emperors of *Blefuscu* did frequently expostulate by their Embassadors, accusing us of making a Schism in Religion, by offending against a fundamental Doctrine of our great Prophet *Lustrog*, in the fifty-fourth Chapter of the *Brundecral* (which is their *Alcoran*). This, however, is thought to be a meer Strain upon the Text: For the Words are these; *That all true Believers shall break their Eggs at the convenient End*: and which is the convenient End, seems, in my humble Opinion, to be left to every Man's

perience that precisely the greatest services to a country engender suspicion and hostility in the monarch and his envious ministers. He helps the Lilliputians to win a victory over the neighboring kingdom by roping together and carrying off the ships of the entire enemy fleet. For this he is raised to the highest rank in the kingdom, but at the same time is secretly charged with being at heart a Big-Endian because he has refused the emperor's request to completely subjugate the people of Blefuscu. "Of so little weight are the greatest Services to Princes, when put into the Ballance with a Refusal to gratify their Passions."[44] A terrible fate is being prepared for him, and he escapes it only by cunning.

There is a sly deftness to all of Swift's writing. The satire is unobtrusively smuggled in amid lush narration and descriptive detail, and there are frequently several levels of meaning within the satire itself. The grotesque possibilities implicit in the disparities of size, first in Lilliput and later in Brobdingnag, are amusingly exploited. For example, one of Gulliver's services to the Lilliputians is his saving of the empress' burning palace by making water on it. But rather understandably, the empress takes this amiss, and becomes his irreconcilable enemy.

The pigmies are suspicious and spiteful, the giants friendly and generous. Hence the giants' kingdom of Brobdingnag is far closer to a true utopia. Whereas the present conditions among the Lilliputians bear a farcical resemblance to Swift's contemporary Europe, the satire in the second part derives chiefly from the direct contrast between European follies and the rationality and

---

Conscience . . . to determine" (Part I, Chap. IV). This whimsical parody is as pertinent today as it was in the age of murderous religious conflicts.

[44] Part I, Chap. V.

wisdom of the king of the giants. This point is made through Gulliver's conversations with the king, who wants to know something about the English constitution and political practices. Gulliver supplies this information with a pretense of patriotism: "Imagine with thy self, courteous Reader, how often I then wished for the Tongue of *Demosthenes* or *Cicero*, that might have enabled me to celebrate the Praise of my own dear native Country in a Style equal to its Merits and Felicity."[45] The satire unfolds to its full extent in the king's reaction to this account. His probing questions repeatedly trip up Gulliver. Thus the king asks what methods are used to train the minds and bodies of the young nobles, and how they spend the early part of their lives, when they are still pliable; what special abilities are asked of those who are raised to new lordships; whether the sovereign's whim, a gift of money to a minister or a lady of the court, or the desire to strengthen a given party which is opposed to the public interest play any part in such promotions, and so on.

> He laughed at my odd kind of Arithmetick (as he was pleased to call it) in reckoning the Numbers of our People by a Computation drawn from the Several Sects among us in Religion and Politicks. . . . He was perfectly astonished with the historical Account I gave him of our Affairs during the last Century, protesting it was only an heap of Conspiracies, Rebellions, Murders, Massacres, Revolutions, Banishments, the very worst Effects that Avarice, Faction, Hypocrisy, Perfidiousness, Cruelty, Rage, Madness, Hatred, Envy, Lust, Malice, or Ambition could produce.[46]

And although Gulliver, in "laudable Partiality" to his own country, artfully eluded many of the king's ques-

---

[45] Part II, Chap. VI.   [46] Part II, Chap. VI.

tions "and gave to every Point a more favourable turn by many Degrees than the strictness of Truth would allow," the truth of the matter cannot be glossed over. The king sums up the results of their conversations: "you have made a most admirable Panegyrick upon your Country. . . . But . . . I cannot but conclude the Bulk of your Natives to be the most pernicious Race of little odious Vermin that Nature ever suffered to crawl upon the Surface of the Earth."[47]

Thus the king's noble and rational principles, apparent in his questions, become the foil for the reality of England. To that extent, utopia and satire here converge— a preparation for the still more general, cruelly perfect satirical utopia in the fourth part of the *Travels*. But in creating his giants Swift anticipates still another theme for satire, one which will dominate the third voyage. In inventing the Lilliputians, Swift is already responding to the new scientific discoveries. For these miniature creatures are not the traditional dwarfs of fairy tales. Their scale vis-à-vis men is small. They go far beyond the possibilities of human tininess; rather, they have the character of human insects,[48] especially in the mass, or even of Leeuwenhoek's "animalcules." A knowledge of the microscopic world seems to have entered into their very conception. This theme is further developed when Gulliver is thrown among the giants. Confronted with excessive bigness, Gulliver finds he is equipped with a microscopic, not to say a clinical eye. As we have seen, Thomson praises the mercy of creation in withholding from man's natural eye perception of the hidden and

[47] Part II, Chap. VI.

[48] The king of Brobdingnag has the same feeling about Gulliver: "Then turning to his first Minister . . . he observed how contemptible a Thing was human Grandeur, which could be mimicked by such diminutive Insects as I" (Part II, Chap. III).

underlying conditions of life. But in Gulliver's case that natural protection is removed. The appearance of the most beautiful women is spoiled for him because he cannot help being aware of the texture of their skins;[49] he sees their underlying physical being, their mortal composition, with terrifying clarity. Here Swift, taking his cue from incipient scientific analysis, hints at a process which would reach its peak in the existential experience of the twentieth century.

Gulliver's other senses, too, especially his sense of smell, acquire the same sort of microscopic acuteness as his vision. Thus he suffers from the intense body odor of the pretty ladies of the court when they pick him up like a lapdog and play lascivious games with him.[50] Then there is the horrifying impression of sick bodies (of a cancerous breast, for example) or of various vermin on clothes and other surfaces, which would pass unseen by an eye of commensurate size. All these sights horrify and

[49] "This made me reflect upon the fair Skins of our *English* Ladies, who appear so beautiful to us, only because they are of our own size, and their Defects not to be seen but through a Magnifying-Glass, where we find by Experiment that the smoothest and whitest Skins look rough and coarse, and ill coloured" (Part II, Chap. I).

[50] "They would often strip me naked from top to toe, and lay me at full Length in their Bosoms; wherewith I was much disgusted; because, to say the Truth, a very offensive Smell came from their Skins; which I do not mention or intend to the Disadvantage of those excellent Ladies . . . ; but, I conceive that my Sense was more acute in proportion to my Littleness, and that those Illustrious Persons were no more disagreeable to their Lovers, or to each other, than people of the same Quality are with us in *England*. . . . The handsomest among these Maids of Honor, a pleasant froliksome Girl of sixteen, would sometimes set me astride upon one of her Nipples, with many other Tricks, wherein the Reader will excuse me for not being over particular" (Part II, Chap. V).

disgust him. Gulliver has already noted the same sensations in a Lilliputian whom he brings close to his body; the small creature discovers that Gulliver's skin is full of holes which display a variety of unpleasant, changing hues. And so forth.

By pursuing the problem of size in such detail, Swift's satire begins to assume that fierce, diabolical character and that universal application which it attains in the fourth part. There the satire is no longer directed at particular social evils, but at the precarious state of human existence in general. Gulliver becomes man himself poised between the worlds of the extremely small and the extremely large—in fact, between the infinite and the infinitesimal. The alternation of perspectives exposes the relativity of all relationships and the immeasurability of their continuous gradations.[51] In all of this we can detect that expansion of consciousness ushered in by the new scientific discoveries and inventions.

The third part of *Gulliver's Travels*, with its descriptions of a miscellany of island peoples, has generally been viewed as an inessential, weaker insertion into the book. To my mind this view is very wrong. The section adds a horizontal dimension to the vertical dimensions in which human limits are exceeded in the other parts. Here Swift selects professional abilities and individual functions out of the human totality and shows how each of these can degenerate. He explores the potentialities of reaching beyond ordinary human lifetimes and human ways, into immortality, to the ghosts of history. This part is, in fact, the most contemporary part of the book for us.

[51] "Undoubtedly Philosophers are in the right when they tell us, that nothing is great or little otherwise than by Comparison. It might have pleased Fortune to let the *Lilliputians* find some Nation, where the People were as diminutive with respect to them, as they were to me" (Part II, Chap. I).

It contains astonishing prophecies of some of the most recent experimentation, and of the quantitative approach that is dominant nowadays. There is, first of all, the flying island of Laputa, a kind of satellite on which dwell the mathematicians who rule the common folk on the land beneath. These are beings who have one eye turned inward, the other upward toward the zenith, and who are so absorbed in their meditations that they need an intermediary with a flyswatter to bring about a connection between them and their surroundings. When they are supposed to listen, he swats them on the ear; when they are to speak, he swats them on the mouth. "Their Ideas are perpetually conversant in Lines and Figures. If they would, for Example, praise the beauty of a Woman . . . they describe it by Rhombs, Circles, Parallelograms, Ellipses, and other Geometrical Terms. . . ."[52]

Their ears are attuned to the music of the spheres, but for all the superrationality of their higher mathematics they are "very bad Reasoners," that is, they completely lack common sense:

> And, although they are dextrous enough upon a Piece of Paper in the management of the Rule, the Pencil and the Divider, yet in the common Actions and behaviour of Life, I have not seen a more clumsy, awkward, and unhandy People, nor so slow and perplexed in their Conceptions upon all other Subjects, except those of Mathematiks and Musick . . . Imagination, Fancy, and Invention, they are wholly strangers to, nor have any Words in their Language by which these Ideas can be expressed.[53]

Here is the perfect caricature of the modern technician.

[52] Part III, Chap. II.

[53] Part III, Chap. II. Their women behave accordingly: "The Women of the Island have abundance of Vivacity . . . and are exceedingly fond of Strangers, whereof there is always a con-

Further, there is the description of the Academy of Projectors in the capital city on the earth below. This is a delicious parody of the Royal Society. A good many of the projects described are actually based on those reported in the Royal Society's journal, *Philosophical Transactions*.[54] Some are sheer jokes, but even these have turned out to be not altogether farfetched. There is, for example, one solemn paper entitled "Extracting Sunbeams out of Cucumbers which were to be put into Vials hermetically sealed and let out to Warm the Air in raw inclement Summers."[55] Comic though such a project was at the time, today we would have to recognize that it foreshadows modern researches into photosynthesis, and the serious consideration being given to ways of harnessing solar energy. Other projects, to be sure, have not lost any of their grotesqueness—for instance "an Operation to reduce human Excrement to its original Food, by separating the several Parts, removing the Tincture which

---

siderable Number from the Continent below. . . . Among these the Ladies chuse their Gallants: but the Vexation is, that they act with too much Ease and Security, for the Husband is always so rapt in Speculation, that the Mistress and Lover may proceed to the greatest Familiarities before his Face" (Part III, Chap. II).

[54] Demonstrated by Marjorie Nicolson and Nora M. Mohler in "The Scientific Background of Swift's *Voyage to Laputa*," *Science and Imagination*, pp. 110-154. The authors write: "Swift's is the *reductio ad absurdum* frequently employed by modern satirists who reduce to nonsense scientific papers and doctoral dissertations, not by inventing unreal subjects but—more devastatingly—by quoting actual titles of papers and theses. . . . The 'invention' in Swift's passages usually consists in one of two things: sometimes he neatly combines two real experiments on different subjects . . . at other times Swift carries a real experiment only one step further—and the added step carries us over the precipice of nonsense" (pp. 138-139).

[55] Part III, Chap. V.

it receives from the Gall, making the Odour exhale, and scumming off the Saliva."[56]

Another wild fancy of Swift's was an instrument "for improving speculative Knowledge by practical and mechanical Operations . . . by [this] Contrivance, the most ignorant Person . . . may write both in Philosophy, Poetry, Politicks, Law, Mathematicks, and Theology, without the least assistance from Genius or Study."[57] Does this not bear a resemblance to jokes about the modern computer?

The point of all this is to show the follies of over-developed reason and materiality. To take this road, the satirist implies, endangers man's humanity. Swift's rejection of this avenue for humankind prepares us for the sweeping indictment of human nature as a whole which is still to come.

The climax of the book is the final section on the land of the Houyhnhnms. All the earlier parts have moved toward this, and it sums them up with a drastic, terrifying consistency. What is depicted here is the most audacious overstepping of human limits. Indeed, it is more than that; the whole realm of humanity has been overturned. The standard of measurement is wrested entirely from man, and transferred to a noble beast that employs detestably depraved, apelike human beings as domestic animals. The essentially human, rational aspect of man is separated from him and given to an animal imbued with the wisdom of nature.

No writer had ever gone so far before. Since the time of Aesop and Aristophanes, animals had been used in parables to set forth moral lessons. In the *Physiologus*, an early Christian bestiary, certain modes of animal behavior, such as the pelican's sacrifice for its young, were held

[56] Part III, Chap. V.   [57] Part III, Chap. V.

up as examples of Christian virtue. Cyrano de Bergerac (1619-1655), in the "Histoire des Oiseaux" episode in his imaginary voyage to the "Estate du Soleil," approached Swift's view of mankind—and in fact Swift borrowed some details from this tale. Here the traveler is condemned to death by a tribunal of birds because he is a human being,

> . . . a bald animal . . . a chimera conglomerated from all sorts of natures and who frightens all others . . . so stupid and so vain that he persuades himself we have been created solely for his sake . . . who asserts that reasoning is possible only by means of the senses but who nevertheless possesses the feeblest, the slowest and the falsest senses among all Creatures . . . whom Nature, to omit nothing, has created like Monsters, but into whom she has nevertheless instilled ambition to rule over all animals and to exterminate them.[58]

But here the charges against man spring from the aversion felt toward him by the animals who are his victims. Although the prisoner is generously pardoned at the intercession of a parrot whom he had freed from its cage on earth, the zoophilic utopia is not pushed to such an extreme as to ascribe true humanity to animals and to man the most bestial of natures. In Cyrano's episode the inhabitants of the Solar State are transformed from birds

[58] ". . . une beste chauve . . . une chimère amassée de toutes sortes de natures, et qui fait peur à toutes . . . si sot et si vain, qu'il se persuade que nous n'avons esté faits que pour luy . . . qui soutient qu'on ne raisonne que par le rapport des sens, et qui cependent a les sens les plus foibles, les plus tardifs et les plus faux d'entre toutes les Créatures . . . que la Nature, pour faire de tout, a créé comme les Monstres, mais en qui pourtant elle a infus l'ambition de commander à tous les animaux et de les exterminer" (Cyrano de Bergerac, *Oeuvres libertines*, ed. Frédéric Lachèvre [Paris, 1921], I, 150).

into spirits, and as such they after all assume ideal human form. Only an uncanny intuition of the human degeneracy latent in the intellectual and technical revolutions of the age could have produced such a terrifying picture as the contrast between the Houyhnhnms, those noble and virtually angelic horses who live in the innocence of primeval reason, and the Yahoos, those men sunk to the depths of baseness.

Gulliver wants to stay on forever in this ideal community of horses. He remembers his native land with a shudder. In his fellow Englishmen he now recognizes the hideous traits of the Yahoos, including those excesses of rationality which he has learned to distinguish from balanced, judicious reason. But his aversion for his own kind extends to the body as well. Expelled from the paradise of noble animals when his host can no longer conceal the fact that he is after all a Yahoo, though an exceptional one, Gulliver returns to mankind. But he finds that he is repelled even by the helpful ship captain who brings him to his native land, and by his wife and children at home—he faints when they kiss him, and it is years before he can bear their presence again.[59]

[59] What Gulliver finds most unbearable about human beings is their arrogance: "My Reconcilement to the *Yahoo*-kind in general might not be so difficult, if they could be content with those Vices and Follies only, which Nature hath entitled them to. I am not in the least provoked at the Sight of a Lawyer, a Pick-pocket, a Colonel, a Fool, a Lord, a Gamester, a Politician, a Whore-master, a Physician. . . . [Note the implicit contempt in this egalitarian catalogue!] This is all according to the due Course of Things: But when I behold a Lump of Deformity, and Diseases both in Body and Mind, smitten with *Pride*, it immediately breaks all the Measures of my Patience. . . . The wise and virtuous *Houyhnhnms*, who abound in all Excellencies that can adorn a Rational Creature, have no Name for this Vice in their Language, which hath no Terms to express any thing that

The island of the Houyhnhnms is a genuine utopia, an imaginary model community like Rabelais' Abbey of Theleme; but Swift has woven into his account the deadliest of satires upon the human race. As we have noted, among the Lilliputians utopian conditions were a thing of the past and the satire was implicit in the picture of the present degenerate institutions, which mirrored European conditions all too closely. The kingdom of the giants has a certain utopian cast, and the social criticism of England is developed in Gulliver's dialogue with the wise king. But the narrator's experience with the relativity of magnitudes and conditions already harbors an ironic comment on the entire human race. In the negative utopias of the third part, the irony is directed against the debasement of specific human qualities. Among the Houyhnhnms, finally, authentic utopia and satire form a unity, each interpenetrating the other.

In *Gulliver's Travels*, then, a wide variety of traditions and tendencies are welded into a unitary, inherently organized structure. It might be well to list these. First, there is the ancient tradition of the travel romance, the

---

is evil, except those whereby they describe the detestable Qualities of their *Yahoos*, among which they were not able to distinguish this of Pride, for want of thoroughly understanding Human Nature, as it sheweth itself in other Countries, where that Animal presides" (Part IV, Chap. XII). Among the Houyhnhnms, innocent creatures of nature that they are, self-consciousness has not yet split off from consciousness. But Gulliver's passionate hatred of humanity leads him into a contradiction: On the one hand nature and reason are identical in the Houyhnhnms; on the other hand he speaks of the "Vices and Follies . . . which Nature has entitled them [the Yahoos] to." What he has earlier condemned as a perversion of nature is now seen as the essential nature of the Yahoos. The inconsistency merely expresses a further degree of furious rejection.

imaginary journey which goes back to the mythic voyage of Odysseus. That tradition has had innumerable off-shoots, the journeys being set both in exotic quarters of the world and in imaginary realms. The tradition has also lent itself to parody. But parody is only one aspect of the universal satiric urge, which ranges freely over all fields and does not limit itself to social criticism, but often penetrates to the depths of human nature. Secondly, there is the equally ancient tradition of utopia, the wish-fulfillment dream of an ideal isle of the blessed. Thirdly, there is the animal fable, a subdivision of which is the ghost story. Fourthly, there is the new scientific point of view, its discoveries and inventions, its analytic and abstracting methods, and its results: the awareness of human relativity and the sense of infinity, openness to the universe, breakthrough beyond the boundaries of humanity. Finally, there is the movement toward totally free thought, a movement both libertarian and libertine. The attitude which in Milton was disguised within the cloak of a Christian epic comes to light, in Swift, in a transparent parable. Milton had already embodied human freedom in his Satan; but Swift goes beyond this to represent the nobility of uncorrupted reason in an animal. For all his espousing of the classic humane values and his rejection of materialism, this Dean of St. Patrick's nevertheless stands squarely in the tradition of the freethinkers of the sixteenth and seventeenth centuries, from Geoffroy Vallée (burned in 1574) to Cyrano de Bergerac. On the other hand, one line of descent from Swift leads to the philosophical novels of Voltaire and, further on, to Rousseau's indictment of civilization. Indeed, Swift anticipates and surpasses Rousseau. Amid all the resplendence of the rising Enlightenment he remains the earliest and at the same time the most radical of the "cultural pessimists."

All these elements are fully integrated in *Gulliver's Travels*. Within that novel a new consciousness was taking form, one which was to be the culture-medium of Romantic consciousness.

Still another ingredient, an extremely fertile and potent one, was added to the medium: the release of human emotionality, the differentiation and intensification of sentiment. In Germany, to be sure, this degenerated into the literary movement called *Empfindsamkeit*, which made sentimentality into a cult. But this development also occurred in England and in France, where it took different directions. In England it sprang principally from the moral conflicts and self-examination of the Puritan soul. In France, where it was more spontaneous and seemed to vary more with individuals, it arose out of the incipient self-disgust and longing for innovation on the part of the nobility and its intellectual dependents. It seems also to have been accompanied by a good deal of self-repudiation. For example, there was Perrault's eulogy in 1687 to the age of "Louis le Grand," which spelled an end to the dominance of classical antiquity. This led to a general liberation from the constraint of rules, a liberation of speech, feeling, and thought, which was ultimately to shake the ancien régime itself. Scientific developments, disseminated by Fontenelle, played a considerable part in all of this. Their effect was to turn men's attention to contemporary phenomena, to stimulate direct observation and experience. The seventeenth century thus was a time when *ratio* became dominant, both socially and philosophically. It was viewed as a force for heroic self-control; we have seen its supreme manifestation in the *Princesse de Clèves*, where *ratio* is equated with human dignity. But at the same time *ratio* was also inspiring criticism of political and religious orthodoxies. It was ultimately to breed doubts of its own power. Massilon, Bishop of Clermont under the Regency, complained that godlessness had actually become a badge of distinction which entitled people to access to the great and raised them above low birth. In the narratives of the eighteenth century, beginning with *Manon Lescaut* (published in 1733) and the *Vie de Marianne* (1731-1741), passion and emotion break through all the traditional barriers. And Madame du Deffand could write to Horace Walpole: "Ah, reason, reason! . . . What power does it have? . . . When may we heed it? What good does it do us? It dominates the passions? That is not true."[60] The doctrines of Rousseau, finally, in themselves show the shift from rationality to originality. Rousseau uses rationalistic methods to fight for the acceptance of natural sentiment.

Thus a movement against the conventions began, directed as much against social conventions as against the conventions of form in the arts. Everywhere, there is a visible effort to achieve direct personal expressiveness. The entire age is seized by the desire to throw off impositions from outside and from the past. Initially, of course, this urge shows up largely in matters of detail,

---

[60] Letter of 23 May 1767: "Ah la raison, la raison! . . . quel pouvoir a-t-elle? . . . quand est-ce qu'on peut l'écouter? quel bien procure-t-elle? Elle triomphe des passions? Cela n'est pas vrai" (*Correspondance de la Marquise du Deffand*, ed. M. de Lescure, 2 vols. [Paris, 1865], I, 381f., Letter 212).

Similarly, Marivaux' Marianne writes: "For my part, I think that feeling alone can give us fairly certain information about ourselves, and that we should not too much rely on what our mind tries to tell us after its own fashion . . ." ("Je pense, pour moi, qu'il n'y a que le sentiment qui nous puisse donner des nouvelles un peu sûres de nous, et qu'il ne faut pas trop se fier à celles que notre esprit veut faire à sa guise . . ."; *Vie de Marianne*, Part I, p. 93, in *Romans de Marivaux* [Paris, 1949]).

within the framework of conventional forms. At the outset, narratives of the eighteenth century follow certain traditional models which had already developed into types. *Don Quixote* is the ancestor of many works, from Marivaux' *Pharamon* to the novels of Fielding, Smollett, and Sterne. The picaresque and adventure novel remains a favorite mode (as, for example, in Lesage's *Gil Blas*, in Louvet de Couvray's *Chevalier de Faublas*, in Defoe's *Captain Singleton*, and Prévost's *Mémoires d'un homme de qualité* and *Cleveland*). The adventure novel, a loosely connected series of colorful experiences, often merges with the kindred theme of the imaginary journey. And even a genre as dissimilar in aim as the moral tale sometimes—as in Defoe's *Moll Flanders* and *Lady Roxana*—retains a touch of the picaresque type. Similarly, certain stylistic vestiges of the chivalric romance are incorporated into the adventure novel when, in the later eighteenth century, it passes over into the type of the spine-chilling "Gothic tale."

Even in the specific shape given to these typical themes one basic element recurs. It is a feature that itself suggests the new tendency toward liberation from the conventions. The stories, whatever their intention, describe chiefly the destinies of persons of obscure, low, or illegitimate origins. Moll Flanders is abandoned soon after her birth by a mother who is transported to the colonies for theft; Moll can scarcely remember her first, unstable years. Captain Singleton is carried off by gypsies as a child and lacks a Christian upbringing. Roxana falls into misery because of a dissolute husband. Richardson's Pamela is a poor servant-girl, Fielding's Tom Jones a foundling. Marivaux' Marianne is orphaned at the age of three when her parents are murdered in a stagecoach; her birth remains obscure. Diderot's nun is the product of her noblewoman mother's adultery, for which reason she becomes the Cinderella of the family and is condemned to the cloister. Such unfortunate beginnings determine the lives of these people, with all their sufferings, their errors, and their atonements. There are a number of reasons for employing such characters: they serve the purpose of social criticism, showing the corruption of both the nobility and the wealthy middle class, or else they are edifying objects, demonstrating as they do the wages of sin and the rewards of repentance. True human virtue, Fielding's "good nature," is set against a hypocritical decorum, true human nobility set against the formal prestige of noble birth.[61]

This stress on humanity and individuality constitutes in itself an internalization of theme. But along with this there is something still more profound. The personal conflicts in the minds and hearts of the three protagonists of the *Princesse de Clèves* involve them alone, within an accepted, inviolate society. The conventions of this society are sacrosanct even to its victims. But now the conflicts acquire an external battlefield; individual spirit-

[61] In Fielding's *Joseph Andrews* there is a scene which is actually a precursor of Maupassant's *Boule-de-suif*. Joseph, robbed by highwaymen and beaten half to death, is lying in a roadside ditch. A stagecoach drives by, and the postilion, moved by the groans of the injured and half-naked man, stops. The passengers invent all sorts of reasons for not taking the poor fellow into the coach. Some are in a hurry; others are afraid of being involved in the affair; a respectable lady refuses to sit in the same vehicle with a naked man. No one is willing to lend the man an extra coat. The only one who does give up the coat he is wearing, and who insists on taking Joseph along after all, is the postilion (a man who is later arrested for stealing chickens), "at the same time swearing a great oath (for which he was rebuked by the passengers), 'that he would rather ride in his shirt all his life, than suffer a fellow-creature to lie in so miserable condition'" (Book I, Chap. XII; text here and below quoted from the Modern Library Edition [New York, 1950]).

ual conflicts become the symbols for class and moral conflicts. Marianne, for example, suffers from the conventions of the nobility and its creatures. She herself is nobler than the nobility in her natural generosity and instinctive sophistication. What drives Clarissa to misfortune is the hypocritical rectitude of a middle class avid for money and position. She herself is a person who takes this moral strictness seriously, to the point of martyrdom. Conventional obstacles intensify personal contradictions, creating a tremendous pressure; the intensity of experience increases correspondingly. This intensity forces expression of feeling precisely in proportion to the weakening of aristocratic self-control over expression. Both internal and external sensitivity grow, bringing a greater awareness of sensual details and psychic impulses. The two are essentially inseparable: in the puritan exercises in the examination of conscience, for example, the smallest details of the milieu acquire importance for the destinies of the soul, and an imponderable influence upon it. It is to this that we owe the painstaking itemization and immoderate length of Richardson's novels.

In France, Marivaux' *Marianne* and *Paysan parvenu* are marked by a sympathetic interest in the life of the lower classes, now viewed for its own sake, without reference to the attitudes of the nobility. What is more, these novels achieve a broader and deeper illumination of both events and feelings.[62] The material takes on a

---

[62] ". . . I felt an astonished pleasure: I was aware of my movements. I was delighted to find myself there. The very air lifted my spirits. There was a sweet sympathy between my imagination and the things around me and I fancied that this multitude of different things would yield joys of a kind I as yet did not know. . . ." (". . . je jouis de toute ma surprise: je sentis mes mouvements, je fus charmée de me trouver là, je respirai un air qui réjouit mes esprits; il y avait une douce sympathie entre mon imagination et les objets que je voyais, et je devinais qu'on

more general significance: the characters are endowed with greater sensibility, with the result that Marianne is forever voicing subtle insights which interrupt the course of the narrative in Proustian fashion.

Above all, the new flexibility and sensitivity in observation makes possible a characterization of persons and settings to an extent scarcely achieved in the novel hitherto. In the *Princesse de Clèves* Madame de La Fayette was concerned solely with outward developments. All three of the exquisitely exemplary characters were sketched in lightly as types, and only the particular constellation formed by these irreproachable persons produced the dialectical entanglement of feelings and the extraordinary conduct of the woman. The aim of the novel was to portray feelings, and to show how they could be mastered by the exercise of human dignity.

In Chaucer, individual characterization was an outgrowth of type traits. Even Furetière's description of the attorney Vollichon, quoted earlier, dwelt less on the characteristics of an individual than on the qualities of a despised profession, down to the typical cap and facial features. Let us now look at a passage from Marivaux' *Vie de Marianne*. We shall see how much has happened in the interval.

> Madame Dorsin was a beautiful woman, but that does not describe her completely. That would not have been the first impression you had of her; you would have been struck by another, more significant quality. . . . Suppose that we were to translate Beauty itself into a human form, and discover that she is somewhat bored at being so committed to being beautiful; that she would rather try her skill at pleasing by other means;

---

pouvait tirer de cette multitude de choses différentes je ne sais combien d'agréments que je ne connaissais pas encore . . ."; *Vie de Marianne*, Part I, p. 89).

that she would want to temper her beauty without losing it; that she would somewhat disguise that quality
by other charms . . . to round out the picture, we
should add that her soul was continually playing over
her features, so that her face expressed all that she felt
and all that she was. Thus she would look as keen, as
delicate, as proud, as serious, as sportive as indeed her
mood was from moment to moment. Now try to imagine the flashes of force, of grace, of sensitivity, and the
endless nuances of changing expression her face would
register. And since we are on the subject of soul, let us
speak further of it. . . . never was there a soul more
nimble than hers, and her mind was no less quick. Most
women of exceptional minds have a certain air of strain,
so that one feels their cleverness is not entirely natural
to them but something assumed. One type will express
herself carelessly in an offhand way, as though to imply
that thought is no trouble to her, that whatever remarkable thing she may have said simply occurred to her.
Another speaks in a cold, serious and decisive manner.
. . . Another is careful to say nothing that is not choice,
and that in a tone even choicer than the comment itself. . . . Madame Dorsin, however, was never guilty of
any of these feminine affectations. The tone in which
she spoke was simply governed by the nature of what
she had to say . . . in fact, I would maintain that her
mind had no specifically sexual cast, although when
Madame Dorsin chose to, she could be the most en-
chantingly feminine of creatures. . . . But Madame Dorsin made use of none of these wiles. She had a kind of
pride which would not let her stoop to them, and which
made her disdain whatever advantages might be won
through them. If in the course of a day she might mo-
mentarily slip into some such fault, she would be the
first to be aware of it. Still, in general, she would much
prefer to be valued for her mental qualities than for her
charms; she did not equate herself with these purely
physical endowments. . . . In truth, she did not mind

one's noticing this contempt she had for all such little
ways of suing favor, and this was the only reproach
which one might level against her, the only form of
coquetry of which she could be accused. Still, of all
frailties, this was surely one of the most forgivable.[63]

[63] "Mme Dorsin était belle, encore n'est-ce pas là dire ce qu'elle
était; ce n'aurait pas été la première idée qu'on eût eue d'elle;
en la voyant, on avait quelque chose de plus pressé à sentir. . . .
Personnifions la beauté, et supposons qu'elle s'ennuie d'être si
sérieusement belle, qu'elle veuille essayer du seul plaisir de
plaire, qu'elle tempère sa beauté sans la perdre, et qu'elle se
déguise en grâces. . . . Ajoutez à présent une âme qui passe à
tout moment sur cette physionomie; qui va y peindre tout ce
qu'elle sent; qui y répand l'air de tout ce qu'elle est; qui la rend
aussi spirituelle, aussi délicate, aussi vive, aussi fière, aussi sérieuse,
aussi badine qu'elle l'est tour à tour elle-même: et jugez
par là des accidents de force, de grâce, de finesse, et de l'infinité
des expressions rapides qu'on voyait sur ce visage. Parlons maintenant
de cette âme, puisque nous y sommes. . . . jamais âme ne
fut plus agile que la sienne, et ne souffrit moins de diminution
dans sa faculté de penser. La plupart des femmes qui ont beaucoup
d'esprit ont une certaine façon d'en avoir qu'elles n'ont pas
naturellement, mais qu'elles se donnent. Celle-ci s'exprime nonchalammant
et d'un air distrait, afin qu'on croie qu'elle n'a
presque pas besoin de prendre la peine de penser, et que tout ce
qu'elle dit lui échappe. C'est d'un air froid, sérieux et décisif que
celle-la parle. . . . Une autre s'adonne à ne dire que des choses
fines, mais d'un ton qui est encore plus fin que tout ce qu'elle
dit. . . . Mme Dorsin ne débitait rien de ce qu'elle disait dans
aucune de ces petites manières de femme: c'était le caractère de
ses pensées qui réglait bien franchement le ton dont elle parlait
. . . et je crois que vous m'entendrez, si je vous dis qu'ordinairement
son esprit n'avait point de sexe, et qu'en même temps ce
devait être de tous les esprits de femme le plus aimable, quand
Mme Dorsin voulait. . . . toutes ces singeries n'étaient point à
l'usage de Mme Dorsin; elle avait une fierté d'amour-propre qui
ne lui permettait pas de s'y abaisser, et qui la dégoutait des avantages
qu'on en peut tirer; ou, si dans la journée elle se relâchait
un instant là-dessus, il n'y avait qu'elle qui le savait: mais, en
général, elle aimait mieux qu'on pensât bien de sa raison que de
ses charmes; elle ne se confondait pas avec ses grâces. . . . A la

The description goes on for pages. Marianne compares Madam Dorsin to her other and real benefactress, Madam de Miran, to whom she is attached with the even greater tenderness she would feel toward a mother. Both women are kindly and helpful to the limits of their natures, but Madam de Miran's limits are set more narrowly by the "mediocrity of her lights; her mind restricted the goodness of her heart." Madam Dorsin's imagination gives her a greater capacity: "her mind pierced to everything you did not dare to tell her; it was the teacher of her heart . . . and gave that heart, on your behalf, every degree of goodness you needed."[64] Here we have the characterization of an individual, a unique figure, in no sense typical, and in no sense dependent on the narrator; a characterization grasped by an objective eye that has concentrated particularly upon the task. Not casual observation but artistic effort is present here. "All these portraits cause me trouble," Marianne writes. "A portrait can be sketched in a few words, but to draw in the exact details . . . is an endless task."[65] In scarcely any previous work can we find so fully conscious and articulated a statement of that passion for expression and the desperate urge to describe the indescribable which is the mark of the true artist:

---

verité, ce dégout qu'elle avait pour tous ces petits moyens de plaire, peut-être était-elle bien aise qu'on le remarquât; et c'était le seul reproche qu'on pouvait hasarder contre elle, la seule espèce de coquetterie dont on pouvait la soupçonner. . . . c'est du moins de toutes les faiblesses la plus honnête . . ." (Part IV, pp. 248-250).

[64] ". . . tout ce que vous n'osiez lui dire, son esprit le pénétrait; il en instruisait son coeur . . . et lui donnait pour vous tous les degrés de bonté qui vous étaient nécessaires" (Part V, p. 254).

[65] "Tous ces portraits me coûtent. . . . On peut ébaucher un portrait en peu de mots; mais le détailler exactement . . . c'est un ouvrage sans fin" (Part IV, p. 248; Part V, p. 258).

When I say that I am going to give you a portrait of
these two ladies, I mean that I shall show you some of
their traits. I would not know how to render what people are in their entirety; at least it does not seem to me
possible to do this. I know the persons with whom I
live much better than I could describe them; there are
things in them that I cannot sufficiently single out in
order to express them, and which I perceive only for
myself and not for others. Or else, if I were to express
them, I would express them badly; there are matters of
feeling so complicated, so delicately precise, that they
become all confused as soon as reflection intervenes.
Then I no longer know where to take hold of them in
order to express them; so that they are in me without
my possessing them.⁶⁶

The power of discrimination at work here is of the
highest order. There is nothing regimented about it. It
moves from physiognomy into the interior of the person,
into the complexity of a character. For the first time in
the history of narrative the storytellers have seen the
internal structure of an individual personality.⁶⁷ Such insights are particularly sharp in the case of such characters

⁶⁶ "Quand je dis que je vais vous faire le portrait de ces deux
dames, j'entends que je vous en donnerai quelques traits. On ne
saurait rendre en entier ce que sont les personnes; du moins cela
ne me serait pas possible; je connais bien mieux celles avec qui
je vis que je ne les définirais; il y a des choses en elles que je ne
saisis point assez pour les dire, et que je n'aperçois que pour moi,
et non pas pour les autres: ou, si je les disais, je les dirais mal: ce
sont des objets de sentiment si compliqués et d'une netteté si
délicate qu'ils se brouillent dès que ma réflexion s'en mêle; je ne
sais plus par où les prendre pour les exprimer; de sorte qu'ils
sont en moi, et non pas à moi" (Part IV, pp. 208-209).

⁶⁷ It is true that, as in the case of classical tragedy, this development was anticipated in the drama: in *King Lear*, in *Hamlet*,
in *Richard II* and *Henry V*, Shakespeare portrayed the profound transrational and transmoral coherence of characters.

as Marianne, Manon, Pamela, and Lovelace, and in the French princes and courtiers depicted by Saint-Simon in his memoirs (written 1694-1749) or by Marie de Sévigné in her letters (a selection of which was first published in 1720). Although the moral or socio-critical intention may color these characters favorably or unfavorably, insight willy-nilly penetrates more deeply, perceiving the connection between good and evil. Of course a standpoint beyond good and evil has not yet been attained; Christian and humanistic values still operate forcefully, and observation is governed by them, works from within them and not above them. But a scoundrel is not only and not absolutely a scoundrel; an angel is not an entirely pure angel. Pamela's virtue is not without a touch of feminine cunning; in fact, her steadfastness is actually a means by which she achieves the marriage to her master. And even Marianne employs her charms cleverly; her virtue—which here is an aspect of free human dignity, not something dictated by religion, as in England—her virtue is one of the charms with which she operates. But above all—and this is the crucial thing and the new thing—these persons (Marianne and Lovelace as well) try to face up to their own natures, to admit the truth to themselves, to be honest with themselves.[68] Consciousness of the self splits off from the individual life with its compulsions and acts. The inner struggles no longer take place upon a single psychological plane, but rather between various strata of the psyche. In England it is moralistic, puritanical self-examination that sets this process in motion; in France it is human sensibility itself.

[68] They are concerned with their entire individual natures; that is the difference from earlier introspection, which was directed chiefly toward temporary mental states and motivations.

THE LIBERATION of sentiment in the eighteenth century, and the insights resulting
from that liberation, altered the forms of
expression. These altered forms of expression in turn further loosened the constraints upon sentiment and self-
reflection. Forms as well as themes overstepped the
bounds of convention. The ego engaged in monologue
and in dialogue became the vehicle of the new narrative.
That is to say, first-person narrative and epistolary narrative became the new techniques for revealing and ex-
ploring the psyche.

First-person narrative is ancient, of course. It arises
quite naturally out of any account of personal experiences, and as such has been employed since classical antiquity in epic writing, memoirs, and meditations. But at
the beginning of the eighteenth century it took on a totally different character. In *Simplicissimus*, for instance,
and in *Gil Blas* as well, it simply serves to communicate
a series of loosely connected autobiographical events and
adventures. But in *Moll Flanders* and *Roxana*, and to
some extent even in *Robinson Crusoe*—to the extent that
a moralizing intention mingles with sheer storytelling—
first-person narrative undergoes internalization. It becomes confession, and as such unstops the springs of the
inner life. We have already been given proof of the shattering power of confession in the earliest document of
the type, St. Augustine's *Confessions*.[1] To be sure, the

[1] The *Meditations* of Marcus Aurelius are merely an account
of Stoic ethics.

confession is still strictly religious in nature. Nevertheless, the drama of conversion wrings from this man of
fierce instincts a degree of self-knowledge unique for his
age. The Augustine of the *Confessions* is drawn primarily as a penitent Christian, subject and object of the
divine scheme of salvation, not an ordinary person of this
earth. This might also be said of the protagonist of a later
story of conversion, John Bunyan's *Grace Abounding*.
On the other hand Rousseau's *Confessions* (written
1765-1770), unencumbered by a religious purpose, are
the first confessions of a purely personal ego, whose aim
is to provide an example of unvarnished truth and painfully acquired self-understanding. Rousseau was quite
cognizant of the uniqueness of his undertaking. In the
preface he writes: "Here is the only portrait of a man
painted exactly according to nature, and in all its truth,
that exists or probably ever will exist. Whoever you are,
whom my destiny or my trustfulness has made the judge
of this work, I adjure you by my misfortunes, by your
compassion, and in the name of the whole human race,
not to destroy a useful and unique work which may
serve as a model for the study of man, which as yet has
scarcely begun."[2]

The confessions of St. Augustine were a form of self-
repudiation, repudiation of the pagan within his own
soul. But the confessions of Rousseau, in keeping with
their altered, internalized meaning, are self-revelations.

[2] "Voici le seul portrait d'homme, peint exactement d'après
nature et dans toute sa vérité, qui existe et qui probablement
existera jamais. Qui que vous soyez, que ma destinée ou ma con-
fiance ont fait l'arbitre de ce cahier, je vous conjure par mes
malheurs, par vos entrailles, et au nom de toute l'espèce humaine,
de ne pas anéantir un ouvrage utile et unique, lequel peut servir
de première pièce de comparaison pour l'étude des hommes, qui
certainement est encore à commencer . . ." (*Les Confessions*
[Paris, 1926]).

They lay bare the whole man in a totally unsparing manner. The sense of dignity which automatically set limits to all previous revelation of the self, a sense at once naïve and aristocratic, is thrown to the winds. Rousseau's confessions expose strata of the psyche which hitherto shame and the requirements of public decorum had hidden from full consciousness. Inevitably, Rousseau was wrong in thinking that no one would ever follow his course. Nowadays we are used to quite other things; compared to Jouhandeau's *Chroniques maritales*, the *Confessions* seem a very mild form of exhibitionism. But they certainly made a breakthrough to that boldness of self-expression for which the narratives of the eighteenth century had been preparing the way.

But first-person narrative altered other things besides outright confession. In France, the eruption of sentiment gave new meaning to that kind of narrative. The Chevalier Des Grieux relates his life not as a series of episodic events, but as the story of his fateful love for Manon, which is the key event of his life. He tells only the outward happenings, but the indissoluble bond between these two persons, which persists through all the whims and accidents of destiny, lends to these happenings a sober gravity and depth. The *Vie de Marianne*, which is stylistically much more important and which really inaugurates the new era, achieves this depth in a different way. The novel is the fragmentary life story of a girl who as the result of a crime has lost her parents and, even more fatefully, all traces of her origins. Supported by real and hypocritical benefactors, she ekes out a precarious existence until a love affair throws her into the company of nobles. At this point the basic theme of the book is sounded: the conflict between nobility by nature and nobility of name. The love story with its concomitant intrigues really plays an incidental part. Marianne is less concerned about her inconstant lover than about his mother, in whom she has won a mother of her own. In losing him she fears that she will lose the mother. The situation is more important than the whole plot. There is a hidden but unmistakable antagonism toward the church and class morality; toward the cleric who is full of preachments but cannot help, and who turns Marianne over to a lustful hypocrite; toward the nuns who lend themselves to the depravities of the powerful; toward the society ladies who want to force the poor girl into an inferior marriage or into a convent. All these characters contrast darkly with the two benefactresses, Madame de Miran and Madame Dorsin, who risk their prestige for Marianne. The ladies of good family show up badly even in comparison to the vulgar little seamstress with whom Marianne boards, who nevertheless possesses a generous heart beneath her clumsy coarseness.

But even this new picture of man's outward situation within the framework of a given time is of small importance in comparison with another innovation in this novel. I mean the illumination of hidden recesses within man and the individual, which are discovered by a process of association. Marianne tells her story in the form of letters to an unnamed friend. In the course of her tale the narrator is frequently led into auxiliary reflections, for which she always apologizes to the recipient. These reflections, although communicated to the friend, are actually addressed to her own ego; they represent an effort to come to terms with the events of her life and with herself. In these passages the narrator is suddenly alone with herself. The dialectic of the emotions, which had already reached considerable development in *La Princesse de Clèves*, has been made even more pertinent by the first-person narrative. In summing up the psychic state, that dialectic occasionally assumes the form of soliloquy; there is here a first hint of interior monologue, or rather, of stream of consciousness.[3] And such reflection then leads to observations of the self and to distinctions such as the following. Marianne discovers her wealthy patron's wicked intentions; the man had first represented himself as an unselfish protector. Her pride demands that, in spite of her poverty, she bring herself to return his presents, and she begins packing the finery he has sent her.

Meanwhile, the packing proceeded, and it will amuse you to hear that in the midst of these noble and courageous thoughts I could not help looking at this underlinen while I was folding it, and saying to myself (but in so low a voice that I could scarcely hear myself): All the same it's well chosen. That meant: What a pity to part with it. A small regret that slightly dishonored my proud indignation, but what can you expect? . . . Great acts are difficult: no matter how much pleasure you take in doing them, there is even greater pleasure in not doing them—I say this jokingly about myself. But in general, it's essential to gather all one's forces to be great; one need only remain as one is to be small. . . . I let myself drop sadly into a chair and said: Oh, how unhappy I am! Dear God, why have you taken my father and my mother from me? Perhaps that was not what I really meant and I spoke about my parents only to make the reason for my sorrow more honorable. Because sometimes we are vainglorious about ourselves; we commit acts of cowardice we don't want to know about, and disguise them under other names. So perhaps I was only weeping about my clothes. . . . Anyhow I was not weeping at all then, but still I was none the

---

[3] Cf. *Vie de Marianne*, Part II, pp. 178-185, esp. p. 183: "I am telling you virtually everything that passed through my mind while I was walking" ("Je vous rapporte à peu près tout ce qui me passait dans l'esprit en marchant").

better for it; I was gathering material for weeping. My
soul was informing itself of everything that could sad-
den it; it was familiarizing itself with its troubles; and
that is not the moment for tears. We shed such tears
only after sadness has taken hold of us, scarcely ever
while it is taking hold. . . .[4]

At such a moment, of course, feeling is very close to the
surface and can easily break out in tears.

But beyond these fine-grained emotions—the graceful-
ness of expression parallels the subtlety of the feelings—
more penetrating distinctions are achieved, of a kind that
were not possible in earlier narratives, not even in *La*

[4] "Cependant le paquet s'avançait; et ce qui va vous réjouir,
c'est qu'au milieu de ces idées si hautes et si courageuses, je ne
laissais pas, chemin faisant, que de considérer ce linge en le
pliant, et de dire en moi-même (mais si bas, qu'à peine m'enten-
dais-je): Il est pourtant bien choisi; ce qui signifiait: C'est dom-
mage de le quitter. Petit regret qui déshonorait un peu la fierté
de mon dépit; mais que voulez-vous? . . . les grandes actions
sont difficiles: quelque plaisir qu'on y prenne, on se passerait
bien de les faire: il y aurait plus de douceur à les laisser là, soit
dit en badinant à mon égard; mais, en général, il faut se redresser
pour être grand: il n'y a qu'à rester comme on est pour être
petit. . . . je me laissai tristement aller sur un siège, pour y dire:
Que je suis malheureuse! Eh! mon Dieu! pourquoi m'avez-vous
ôté mon père et ma mère? Peut-être n'était-ce pas là ce que je
voulais dire, et ne parlais-je de mes parents que pour rendre le
sujet de mon affliction plus honnête; car quelquefois on est
glorieux avec soi-même, on fait des lâchetés qu'on ne veut pas
savoir, et qu'on se déguise sous d'autres noms; ainsi peut-être
ne pleurais-je qu'à cause de mes hardes. . . . Je ne pleurais pourtant point alors, et je n'en étais pas mieux; je recueillais de quoi
pleurer; mon âme s'instruisait de tout ce qui pouvait l'affliger,
elle se mettait au fait de ses malheurs; et ce n'est pas là l'heure
des larmes: on n'en verse qu'après que la tristesse est prise, et
presque jamais pendant qu'on la prend . . ." (Part III, pp. 180-
181, 183-184).

Princesse de Clèves. There is, for example, the distinction
between life and existence:

> You will imagine that my chief preoccupation was my
> unhappy situation. But no, that situation concerned only
> my life; and what preoccupied me, concerned me, was
> rather my very self. You will say that I am not lucid
> to make such a distinction. Not at all. Our life is, so to
> speak, less dear to us than ourselves, our passions. Some-
> times, seeing what takes place in our instinct, we are
> tempted to say that it is not necessary to live in order
> to be; that it is only by accident that we live, but that
> it is natural that we exist. One might say, for example,
> that when a man kills himself he departs from life only
> in order to save himself, only to rid himself of an in-
> convenient thing; it is not himself he is trying to shake
> off, but the burden he bears.[5]

In this way, then, first-person narrative becomes semi-
autobiographical narrative. Alongside monologue, dialogue—the epistolary narrative—develops. A story told
in letters is also nothing new in itself. Hellenistic rhetori-
cians (Alciphron and the so-called Aristaenetus) employed epistolary exchange for their erotic tales, in order

---

[5] "L'objet qui m'occupa d'abord, vous allez croire que ce fut
la malheureuse situation où je restais: non, cette situation ne
regardait que ma vie; et ce qui m'occupa me regardait, moi.
Vous direz que je rêve de distinguer cela; point du tout: notre
vie, pour ainsi dire, nous est moins chère que nous, que nos passions. A voir quelquefois ce qui se passe dans notre instinct là-
dessus, on dirait que, pour être, il n'est pas nécessaire de vivre;
que ce n'est que par accident que nous vivons, mais que c'est
naturellement que nous sommes. On dirait que, lorsqu'un homme
se tue, par exemple, il ne quitte la vie que pour se sauver, que
pour se débarrasser d'une chose incommode; ce n'est pas lui dont
il ne veut plus, mais bien du fardeau qu'il porte" (Part III, p.
178).

to achieve a heightened effect by direct statement. And
in the pastoral poetry of the period (for example, in
Aelian's *Peasants' Letters*) letters sometimes served to express the nostalgia of a tired civilization for pure, idyllic
nature—one more illustration of the general rule that as
the ancient world approached its end, it arrived at incipient modern tendencies which it could not pursue further.
Later, too, letters were occasionally used as the vehicles
of narrative; in Germany, from Jörg Wickram* on, the
tendency persisted throughout the baroque period. But
it was not until the eighteenth century that epistolary
narration acquired central importance. Then it revealed
all its potentialities, and gave a powerful impetus to the
internalization of narrative.

As is well known, the originator of this fateful innovation was Samuel Richardson, and the crucial book his
Clarissa Harlowe. The technique did not arise out of deliberate artistic intention; in general Richardson, unlike
Marivaux, was not a conscious artist. He was an unreflec-
tive storyteller who wrote for the interests and edification of his middle-class audience; but he had the imagination of genius, which drove him willy-nilly to ultimate
conclusions about his characters and situations and often
made him soar far above the confines of his moralistic
intentions. Even Richardson's criticism of the upper
bourgeoisie is inadvertent, with him; it arises out of the
theme itself, out of the contrasts among individuals, and
out of moralistic rather than socio-critical intentions. The
ultimate model and framework of his novels remains the
English moral tale. Just as in Defoe the didactic tendency
served as a cover for bawdry, so in Richardson all sorts
of unsavory materials are concealed beneath the stern

* A native of Colmar, fl. middle of the sixteenth century, considered the originator of the German novel.—Tr.

puritanical morality, materials that are, of course, promptly disavowed after they are set forth.

By trade Richardson was a successful printer. He was fifty-one years old when he was asked to compose a book of model letters for the use of people who could not write their own. The project stimulated him, and along with *The Complete Letter Writer* he turned out his great epistolary novels, *Pamela* (1740), *Clarissa* (1747-1748), and *Sir Charles Grandison* (1753-1754). Even his masterpiece, *Clarissa*, does not entirely deny its humble origins. And moving though it is, viewed superficially it has the trappings of the cheap sensational novel: cruel family, abduction by a diabolic seducer, incarceration in a house of ill fame, violation, a father's curse, and triumph of virtue at the end. But in its substratum the story is not so simple.

Clarissa is in every respect a monstrous book, combining the crassest contrasts and the most contradictory elements. But it fuses them into a single, clear, inwardly coherent theme. It has come a long way from the loose serial construction of the adventure novel.

In sheer bulk the book is also monstrous, like all of Richardson's novels. Its size is a natural consequence of the urge to exploit to the full all the potentialities of epistolary technique. And that technique particularly suited the bourgeois public's craving for facts and the puritan fondness for poking into the recesses of the soul. The epistolary technique also freed Richardson from the strict use of orderly narrative form, whereby the story had to be told according to the order of events. Now the psychological undercurrents of the events could be revealed even more easily than in the new first-person novel. Feelings pour out immediately and in the present, addressed to a particular person. Relieved of the obligation to abide by strict narrative sequence, the human being can show himself less artificially. In Richardson's epistolary novels narration is mingled with exclamations, complaints, maledictions, discussions of the situation; descriptions are interrupted, continued, bypassed; and in the narrative portions themselves, as they proceed from day to day, all the petty circumstances and ramifications of events, together with the accompanying dialogues, are recorded. Partly because of the greater immediacy of expression and the imaginary presence of a definite addressee, partly because the narrator imposes no constraints on himself, the letter form is almost more untrammeled than the confession, which is directed toward the depths of the past and addressed to an anonymous recipient. In the circles of the nobility this total abandonment of discipline in expression was regarded as shameless. The reaction of the English aristocrat Lady Mary Wortley Montagu is typical when she speaks of Clarissa's "maxim of declaring all she thinks to all the people she sees, without reflecting that in this mortal state of imperfection, fig-leaves are as necessary for our minds as our bodies, and 'tis as indecent to show all we think, as all we have."[6]

Thus the story lumbers on, freighted with all the minute tremors of the inner life and the responses of the addressee; each step forward follows phases of protracted stagnation. Step by step we participate in the growing unbearableness of the situations, until each of the tensions comes to its inevitable explosion. The complex forward movement on a broad front delays the narrative, but also makes it more flexible; the slowness both fatigues the reader and sharpens the suspense. In fact, what arises out of this provokingly gradual progress is a dramatic tension within the epic flow such as had not hitherto been

[6] Letter of 20 October 1755 to the Countess of Bute (*Letters from Lady Wortley Montagu*, Everyman's Library Edition [London and New York, 1934], p. 466).

achieved (except, in far smaller measure, in *La Princesse de Clèves*). We can clearly sense how Richardson is carried away, from situation to situation, into an ever more intensive presentation of psychological states and into depths of characterization he had never foreseen in his original plan, and whose consequences have slipped from his control. Yet this very process gives a powerful impetus to the narrative.

Such deeper psychological penetration was furthered by another innovation, which the epistolary technique made possible: splitting the point of view. The same event is described by different persons in terms of their special nature, the narrator immersing himself in these characters. The multiple reflections illuminate the characters in their complexity. Lovelace's violent reactions, for example, reveal certain of Clarissa's traits which would not be so apparent from her behavior. Granted, this many-sided presentation is still handled clumsily by Richardson, with insufficient artistic skill. The same details are often pedantically repeated from the other point of view. Letters whose contents have already been reported are subsequently quoted word for word. Paradoxically, however, in all such instances the defects of the technique underline its usefulness. By this amorphous structure Richardson succeeds in showing the deep consistency of fates originating from within the characters. Choderlos de Laclos, a greater artist of lesser force, who rid the epistolary technique of all its excrescences and achieved complete formal mastery of it, failed in his *Liaisons dangereuses* to achieve anything like the fateful if ponderous impact of *Clarissa*.

The technical paradoxes are implicit in the very plot of the novel. For the action leads, by way of a series of the crudest events, to genuine inner compulsions. Clarissa's own character is deeply involved in the frightful acts of violence inflicted upon her. For Marivaux' Marianne the moral struggle consists in maintaining her purity and dignity despite the temptations of her rich patron, M. de Climal, and the intrigues of aristocratic society. With quick instinct she seizes upon whatever expedient comes her way; and as the quoted passages make clear, for all her honesty she does not treat herself pedantically. She allows her feminine nature a certain leeway, thus relieving the psychological pressure upon herself and making it easier for her well-wishers to come to her aid. Moreover, her struggle is external to the extent that she is not inwardly bound by the aristocratic canon that causes her sufferings.

Clarissa's moral struggle is much more profound because it is an inner conflict. She is committed body and soul to the middle-class moral convention of which she is the victim. She is imprisoned within it and accepts all its strictures. Puritan morality rules, both inwardly and outwardly. Family honor; her unconditional obedience, in fact slavish subjugation, to the will of her parents; the most minute rules of propriety—in spite of inevitable resistance on certain occasions, she does not challenge the validity of all these constraints. The curse or blessing of an inhuman father exerts a terrible power over the girl. Reconciliation with her family, who have inflicted intolerable psychological abuse and unmitigated harshness upon her, remains her chief concern until her death. What actually destroys Clarissa is not the diabolical abductor Lovelace, but her family, outside of her and inside of her.

The family is a massive complex. In addition to Clarissa's father and mother and her brother and sister, a whole clan of uncles, aunts, and cousins belong to it and occasionally meet in family council. The guiding spirit is her brother James, a narrow-minded, arrogant young fellow who makes use of the tenets of morality to extend the power and prosperity of the family and thus benefit himself as principal heir. All the other members of the family are subject to his influence, in particular the father, who wields decisive authority.

The groundwork of the tragedy is laid by the enmity, formed at the university, between Clarissa's brother and Lovelace, his superior in intellect and vital force. Lovelace first shows his better side; he is young, handsome, fun-loving, sensitive, impulsive, and engaging. What is more, he enjoys a large income and has certain prospects of inheritance from his wealthy, highly respected family. That is how he is enthusiastically described by Clarissa's elder sister, Annabella, who assumes that his advances are directed toward her. In the brother's absence the Harlowes are by no means indisposed to such an advantageous match. Lovelace's notorious profligacy, they decide, will be subdued by marriage. But Lovelace has his eye on the prettier Clarissa and skillfully maneuvers Annabella into a rejection she does not mean seriously, but which he at once accepts. Thereupon Annabella's infatuation is transformed to jealous hatred. Her brother, after his return, finds her a passionate ally when he incites the family to bitter hostility toward Lovelace. Since Lovelace goes on calling despite the coldest reception, James provokes an encounter. He is wounded by Lovelace and hates him the more for the conciliatory generosity with which Lovelace afterwards treats him.

From the start Clarissa displays exemplary goodness and propriety. In contrast to her sister and her own closest friend, Anne Howe—to whom she writes recounting all that happens—Clarissa shows herself scarcely receptive to Lovelace's persuasive courtship. Undoubtedly Richardson meant to present Clarissa as an angel of innocence and virtue, destined to overcome evil and purify the sinners by her unshakable and incorruptible will. But his imagination involuntarily led him to shatter this moral cliché and to create a character of far greater truthfulness. Of course Clarissa is innocent, as far as her will is concerned, of all the cruelties she is subjected to. But not as far as her nature is concerned, for she is by no means an angel. Her pure will partakes of the Harlowes' haughty obstinacy; Lovelace is right when, in a fit of rage and despair, he calls her a true daughter of the Harlowes. This obstinacy, this integral severity, this remarkable lack of feminine gentleness and feminine susceptibility on the one hand keeps her from succumbing to the seducer, but on the other hand spurs Lovelace's savage instincts to the utmost. The encounter between these two persons is initially nothing more than a crude and in fact obscene meeting between a lecher and a frigid governess. But the resulting psychological entanglement is harrowing to both their natures; Clarissa's frigidity is melted by suffering, and Lovelace actually arrives at a real, purified love. Despite all of his sinfulness, despite his base intrigues and acts of violence, he is fundamentally more human than she.

Clarissa becomes involved in the most innocent fashion in a correspondence with Lovelace. One of her uncles wants information for a young friend from the widely traveled Lovelace, and Lovelace is willing to provide it if Clarissa will serve as intermediary. This businesslike correspondence with its inquiries and replies has taken place under the family's eye. Clarissa has ignored the love notes Lovelace occasionally slips in with his letters. As the hostilities between him and the Harlowes intensify, she believes she must continue the correspondence, in spite of the family ban, in order to keep his dangerous ire in check. Thus the correspondence becomes secret—though she herself has no personal interest in Lovelace. But the family, incited by her brother to hysterical fear of Lovelace and his intentions toward Clarissa, suspect a secret bond. In order to destroy his hopes utterly they decide on a hasty marriage for Clarissa, to a man who is in every respect the diametrical opposite of the dreaded seducer, except that he too promises to bring a great increase in wealth to the family.

There now follows, recounted in letters over hundreds of painful pages tracing all the daily details, the story of Clarissa's martyrdom by her tyrannical family. They are unanimously determined to force the girl to marry this man, whom she detests. By their pressure they actually drive her toward Lovelace. All the thumbscrews of morality, family honor, and filial love are mercilessly applied. Clarissa is kept a prisoner in her room, cut off from all communication with the outside world, deprived of comfort even from the faithful servants. She throws herself imploringly at the feet of each of her relatives in turn—a great deal of throwing oneself at the feet was the rule during this period. She vows to remain unmarried forever if only she will be allowed to escape this husband. All in vain. The family threatens to use legal stratagems to deprive her of her grandfather's legacy; they strip her of all means of self-support.

Throughout the whole bourgeois era, tyrannical fathers and guardians have raged in life as well as in novels and dramas. But the case of Clarissa, which marks the first literary account of this phenomenon, is probably the most extreme. For here it is not just the ruling domestic tyrant, but an entire clan which, individually and as a corporate body, subjects the girl to outrageous humiliations and blackmail to break her will. They do not succeed in breaking it, but neither do they break her unshakable attachment and submission to this family. Clarissa has found ways to smuggle out her forbidden letters to her friend Anne Howe and to Lovelace. Both the friend and Lovelace, whose spies keep him informed, offer their aid. But her fatal goodness causes her to hesitate repeatedly and prevents her from escaping in time on her own initiative. Even when the day of her forced marriage has come very close, she is still convinced that the members of her family will change their minds and show mercy.

After endless vacillation, at the last moment she finally decides to run away with Lovelace. But when all preparations have been made for the abduction, she wants to cancel the whole thing after all. To tell him so, she has to meet him secretly at the garden gate. But Lovelace is determined to put an end to this dangerous shilly-shallying. After vain attempts at persuasion he forces her to flee with him at the last moment, by pretending that they have been discovered. She is never able to forgive him for this ruse. It is his original sin, and her own as well. For neither can she forgive herself for leaving the family, to which she is inwardly indissolubly bound. Until her dying day she agonizes over the thought that they might have yielded if she had stayed. The idea is wholly improbable, but of course the possibility remains. And her own self-reproaches magnify her charges against Lovelace.

And now, largely because of her own scruples, she plunges from one form of coercion into another, from the power of the family into the power of her abductor. The terrible duel between the lecher and the governess begins. Of course Lovelace is not the villain he was taken to be—not only in the world of the English middle class, but throughout the contemporary bourgeois world. He is an extremely complex character, Richardson's real masterstroke. Just as Clarissa was originally planned as an angel, Lovelace was meant to be a devil. At the beginning of the book, in a letter to his friend Belford, there is a boastfully depraved confession in the manner of Shakespeare's Richard III or Schiller's Franz Moor. Lovelace says that in his youth he loved, or thought he loved, a coquette "whose infidelity I have vowed to revenge upon as many of the sex as shall come into my power. I believe, in different climes, I have already sacrificed a hecatomb to my Nemesis, in pursuance of this vow."[7] And he boasts that by means of his double agent he has guided events in the Harlowe household according to his own desires, "permitting so much to be revealed of my life and actions, and intentions, as may give him [Clarissa's brother] such a confidence in his double-faced agent, as shall enable me to dance his employer upon my own wires. . . ."[8]

But even here his wickedness is not unequivocal; even here we feel his human vulnerability and the profound complexities of his character. For the first time, he confesses, he is really in love, and "that love increasing with her—what shall I call it?—'Tis not scorn: 'Tis not pride: 'Tis not the insolence of an adored beauty:—but 'tis to *virtue*, it seems, that my difficulties are owin; and I pay for not being a sly sinner, an hypocrite; for being regardless of my reputation. . . ."[9] Hatred for that obstinate virtue merges with hatred for the hypocritical propriety of the middle-class family. The fact that Clarissa's resistance is not due to another man, but to sheer indifference to his charms, offends his vanity just as much as it increases his ardor; he faces a double challenge. And the motives that gnaw at him from the start, that cause his

[7] Lovelace to Belford, March 13 (the entire narrative takes place in the course of a single year); Vol. I, Letter XXX. The text is quoted from the edition of 1811, ed. Rev. E. Mangin (reprinted in London, 1902).

[8] *Ibid.*   [9] *Ibid.*

whims and impulses to shift incessantly, are a sporting urge to conquer the unconquerable, love of intrigue, vindictiveness toward the Harlowes and toward Clarissa, against both forms of virtue, one false and one true, a rage at the girl's flawlessness and at the same time a growing admiration and love which he cannot control—love and hate at once, each feeding the other: "REVENGE, which I love; . . . LOVE, which I hate, *heartily* hate, because 'tis my master. . . ."[10] These psychological confusions trip him up. He is not cold enough to be a sheer devil; nevertheless love cannot—or rather can only when it is too late—wrench him away from his stereotyped technique of handling women, of which he is so proud. The tricks of the dandy, the Don Juan, the master of intrigue fail him; the bravado becomes desperation, the seducer a hounded, suffering human being.

But it takes, to produce such a development, an antagonist as narrow-minded and unfeeling as Clarissa, utterly obsessed with family and propriety. Freed from the clutches of her family, she will not say a kind word to her wholly respectful rescuer. She showers him with reproaches and reprimands. She does not allow him a single critical remark against her family, even against her abominable brother. She makes it perfectly plain that rapid reconciliation with the family is all she is concerned about; that she subordinates everything else to this and will not marry without her father's consent; that she will throw over Lovelace without a scruple if by doing so she can win the family's forgiveness.[11] She even rejects

---

[10] *Ibid.*

[11] ". . . if the giving him up forever will make my path to reconciliation easy, and if they will signify as much to me, they shall see that I never will be *his*. . . ." To this is added her incredible moral arrogance, which would have infuriated even a less irritable lover: "for I have the vanity to think my soul his

the protection of his powerful relatives, which would probably have shielded her from all the coming evils, because she is afraid that accepting such protection will offend her family. Throughout all this she acts toward Lovelace like an insufferable governess dealing with a naughty pupil; from the start he is a "wicked wretch," a "vile intruder," who must thoroughly reform and pass through a period of moral probation before his suit can be heard. She distrusts him, quite rightly, for he has a savage nature given to uncontrollable passions and cynical intrigues. But in his feeling for her he is a captive, and a Marianne would have known how to seize upon that feeling and use it to tame him by more feminine wiles.[12] Even Clarissa's friend advises her not to strain severity, but to accept without delay the marriage he has tempestuously proposed.[13] Although he is still hatching

---

soul's superior" (Clarissa to Miss Howe, April 22; Vol. III, Letter LIII).

[12] "My charmer, I see, has a pride like my own: but she has no *distinction* in her pride: nor knows the pretty fool that there is nothing nobler, nothing more delightful, than for lovers to be conferring and receiving obligations from each other" (Lovelace to Belford, Vol. III, Letter XXVI).

[13] "Yet, it is my opinion, that you *must* bend a little; for he cannot bear to be thought slightly of" (April 18; Vol. III, Letter XXXVI). "Methinks I see the man hesitating, and looking like the fool you paint him, under your corrective superiority!— But he is not a fool. Don't put him upon mingling resentment with his love" (Vol. III, Letter XIX). ". . . I wish you *could* have taken him at offers so earnest" (Vol. III, Letter LVIII). Miss Howe is wiser in the ways of love than Clarissa. On April 18 she writes: ". . . I think that *smooth* love; that is to say, a passion without rubs; in other words, a passion without passion; is like a sleepy stream that is hardly ever seen to give motion to a straw. So that, sometimes to make us fear, and even, for a short space, to *hate* the wretch, is productive of the *contrary* extreme" (Vol. III, Letter XXXVI).

evil plans to make her his mistress, out of reluctance to enter marriage and for revenge upon the Harlowes, he is really unsure of himself during this early period after the abduction; and his infatuation, which brings him to the point of masochistic self-abasement, makes him prepared for the most restraining of ties.[14] If Clarissa were capable of any real affection she would recognize his vacillations for what they are and be moved by them. Instead she postpones her consent, imposing all sorts of

[14] Clarissa reports on his behavior in her letter of April 15: "O charmer of my heart! snatching my hand, and pressing it between both his, to his lips, in a strange wild way, take me, take me to yourself: mould me as you please: I am wax in your hands; give me your own impression, and seal me for ever yours—We were born for each other!—You to make me happy, and save a soul—I am all error, all crime. . . . include me in your terms: prescribe to me . . . put a halter about my neck, and lead me by it, upon condition of forgiveness on that disgraceful penance, and of a prostration as servile, to your father's presence . . . and I will beg his consent at his feet, and bear any thing but spurning from him, because he is your father. But to give you up upon *cold* conditions, d——n me (said the shocking wretch) if I either will, or can!" (Vol. III, Letter XXIX). And Lovelace himself writes to his friend Belford, with whom he is perfectly frank: "What a miscreant had I been, not to have endeavoured to bring her back, by all the endearments, by all the vows, by all the offers, that I could make her! . . . I was in earnest in my vows to marry, and my ardour to urge the present time was a *real* ardour" (April 24; Vol. III, Letter LX). But on the following day he adds: "But when a man has been ranging, like the painful bee, from flower to flower . . . and the thoughts of home and a wife begin to have their charms with him, to be received by a Niobe, who, like a wounded vine, weeps her vitals away, while she but involuntary curls about him; how shall I be able to bear that? May Heaven restore my charmer to health and spirits, I hourly pray—that a man may see whether she can love any body but her father and mother!" (Vol. III, Letter LXI).

conditions and formalities as barriers, and thus again misses the saving opportunity.[15]

Richardson knots his net of nemesis very finely, tracing its growth from day to day. We cannot follow it in detail here. Given Clarissa's nature, she must repeatedly be driven back into her rigid attitude by the very storminess of Lovelace's courtship. And her rigidity in turn arouses his worst impulses, forcing him to resort to his cynical tricks for dealing with women, driving him to furious, completely superfluous deceptions and acts of violence. Moreover, the deeper he plunges into his machinations, the more difficult it becomes for him to beat a retreat. He responds to the test of virtue she imposes upon him with a reverse test: he will see whether he cannot after all undermine her by trickery, entreaties, and seductions.[16] Clarissa refuses to succumb to him, just

[15] Lovelace to Belford, April 21 (Vol. III, Letter XLVI): "I re-urged her to make me happy; but I was to be postponed to her cousin Morden's arrival" (the one relative—absent in Italy—who she expects may be able to sway the family). Clarissa to Anne Howe, April 26: "Then some *little* punctilio surely is necessary. No preparation made. No articles drawn. No licence ready . . . who could think of entering into so solemn an engagement?" (Vol. III, Letter LVII). And later: "I verily think, that had he urged me again, in a *proper manner*, I should have consented (little satisfied as I am with him) to give him a meeting to-morrow morning at a more solemn place than in the parlour below" (Vol. IV, Letter I). On April 28: "He now does nothing but talk of the *ceremony*, but not indeed of the *day*. I don't want him to urge that—but I wonder he does not" (Vol. IV, Letter IV).

[16] Lovelace to Belford, April 13: ". . . am I not justified in my resolutions of trying *her* virtue, who is resolved, as I may say, to try mine? . . . Wilt thou not thyself . . . allow me to try if I cannot awaken the *woman* in her?—To try if she, with all that glowing symmetry of parts, and that full bloom of

as she refused to succumb to her family. And that intensifies his bitterness until he reaches the point of sheer
brutality. He has lured her to London, lives with her in
a notorious house he has rented for her, and holds her
captive under the guard of his hired creatures. But she
remains untouchable. In his long-winded letters to his
friend we follow the daily vicissitudes of psychological
torture, Clarissa's vain attempts at escape and Lovelace's
abrupt shifts from sadistic coercion to masochistic remorse. All this is as painful to read as her former sufferings at the hands of her family.

At last the drama reaches its extreme: Lovelace drugs
Clarissa and violates her while she is asleep. By that act
he loses her forever. She locks herself in her room, accepts nothing further from him, at last escapes him by a
trick and finds refuge with helpful people. But Richardson does not let it go at that; he pushes her martyrdom
to the utmost. Lovelace's overzealous servants undertake
on their own to pursue their captive, find Clarissa, and
under the pretext that she has not paid her rent send her
to jail. The heartbreaking spectacle of this ultimate hu-
miliation—the stainless Clarissa in the filth of the jail—
prepares the way for the virtual sanctification of her last
moments. Lovelace's friend Belford, who like Miss Howe
has been on Clarissa's side from the start and has been
urging mercy and forbearance, frees her and protects her
from Lovelace. The remainder of the book is devoted to
her fatal physical collapse and spiritual ascent, above the
sufferings of her young life.

The picture of this last redeeming period, moving
though it is, shows Clarissa still—even when she has already passed halfway out of the world—as slavishly sub-

---

vernal graces, by which she attracts every eye, be really inflexible as to the grand article?" (Vol. III, Letter XVIII).

ject as ever to the authority of her family and bourgeois convention. Not even utmost suffering can bring about true release into a realm of pure humanity ("no terror can make her forget her punctilio"). Until the end she humbly begs for the favor of her relatives, for the revocation of her father's curse and the blessing of her parents—who only realize after her death what they have done. Until the end she also remains the stern governess of her lover; she forgives him out of Christian duty, but not from the heart, and his wild repentance, his longing for atonement, leave her completely cold. She has not the slightest inkling of what goes on in his mind and heart.

Kleist's Marchioness of O, who is in a similar situation, accedes to formal marriage to the man who raped her while she was unconscious, and as a result of his good behavior peace is gradually restored between them and a genuine love arises. Clarissa permits no atonement, in spite of the promises of protection from Lovelace's relatives, in spite of the persuasions of her friend. Instead, she lets him simmer in the inferno of his guilt and his unrequited love; her death seems to him a last triumphant act of revenge committed by her indomitable will in their sexual struggle.[17] Here we encounter the insurmountable limitation of Clarissa and her narrator. Richardson en-

---

[17] Lovelace to Belford, September 6: "So this lady, as I suppose, intended only at first to vex and plague me; and . . . her desire of revenge insensibly became stronger in her than the desire of life; and now she is willing to die, as an event which she thinks will cut my heart-strings asunder. And still, the *more* to be revenged, puts on the Christian, and forgives me. But I'll have none of her forgiveness! My own heart tells me I do not deserve it; and I cannot bear it!—And what is it but a mere *verbal* forgiveness, as ostentatiously as cruelly given with a view to magnify herself, and wound me deeper!" (Vol. VIII, Letter LXIX).

dowed his heroine with an organically consistent character; but her apotheosis—inevitably, given the principles
of the author and his audience—remained embedded in
middle-class morality and could not attain to any human
liberation.

Consequently, the end of Lovelace is actually more
moving than that of Clarissa. For in him, at least, a breakthrough to self-knowledge takes place. Lovelace, who
right up to the conclusion of the book remains a man
torn between arrogance and humility, between self-satis-
faction and suffering over his own nature, between unending desire and the longing for purification, comes to
realize that all his maneuvers were wasted on a personality like Clarissa's and that he could probably have won
her by the route of honesty and patience—which, however, he was incapable of taking. *I never lied to man,
and hardly ever said truth to woman. The first is what
all free-livers cannot say: the second what every one
can.*[18] That sentence says everything about his
machismo and his Don Juanism. But, he goes on to complain, "How my heart sickens at looking back [at] what
I was!" And: *"Why, why did my mother bring me up
to bear no controul? Why was I so educated, as that to
my very tutors it was a request that I should not know
what contradiction or disappointment was?*—Ought she
not to have known what cruelty there was in her kindness? . . . the very repentance and amendment, wished
me so heartily by my kind and cross dear, has been inval-
idated and postponed, and who knows for how long?—
the amendment at least; can a madman be capable of
either?"[19] He himself sees to his atonement; he dies in a
chivalric duel with Clarissa's cousin Morden. As he falls,

[18] Vol. IX, Letter XXXIX.
[19] To Belford on the same day (Vol. IX, Letter XXXVIII).

he says to his antagonist: "You have well revenged the dear creature." "I have, Sir," Morden replies, "and perhaps shall be sorry that you called upon me to this work. . . ." Whereupon Lovelace responds: "There is a fate in it! . . . a cursed fate!—or this could not have been!—But be ye all witnesses, that I have provoked my destiny. . . ."[20]

And in fact it is destiny that this novel recounts—for the first time not individual fates, but fate, not a fate imposed from without by a didactic Providence, but the inner concatenation of characters and conditions which drives two human beings to their misfortune. Here we no longer have the simplistic scheme of virtue triumphing over vice, which was the author's original, superficial plan. The moralistic intention has been displaced by the power of psychological development. We see the limitations of the era, of which middle-class morality itself is a part; we see the mistakes of two persons, which sprang from their natures, from the clash of their characters. Clarissa does not know better; Lovelace cannot help himself—that is what produces the fatal outcome. In the *Princess de Clèves* the tragedy sprang from a constellation of emotions among three persons, all of whom were equally excellent, morally on the same plane. The conflict there arose not from the complexities of personalities but from the conflagration of emotions. In *Clarissa*, on the other hand, we are shown the relentless conflict of characters who are delineated in depth, down to their deep social roots. It is evident what a great internalizing innovation in narrative this signifies.

We find this new tendency to characterization, to penetration into specific personalities, not only in *Clarissa*,

---

[20] J. F. De la Tour, who was present at the duel in Trent, to John Belford on December 18 (Vol. IX, Letter LXIII).

but also in the other crucial novels discussed here, in *Manon Lascaut* and the *Vie de Marianne* as well as in the memoirs and letters of the period. It is as if a crypt for the individual psyche were being excavated—a process simultaneously manifested, in the narrator's moralistic reflections and views upon life, as an extension of psychological consciousness. In this process, the techniques of the first-person novel and the epistolary novel are as much symptom as vehicle. The splitting of viewpoint, which the epistolary novel permits, by providing mutual illumination of the characters, brings out and increases their complexity. But the most important impetus to internalization is the psychic and temporal immediacy, the spontaneity and contemporaneity of the narration, ushered in by these two narrative forms. The "I" of confessions and of letters actually signifies the first step in a displacement of the narrative center of gravity from the outside to the inside, a displacement which henceforth continues apace. *The narrator's observation and command post is set up inside, in man's innermost self, and consequently events themselves are more and more shifted to the interior of the narrating ego.*

The additional stock-in-trade provided by the new narratives—amplitude of characterization and emotion—was at once available to the ever-alert English satirists, and they exploited it superbly. The beginning of the process can already be seen in Fielding. For all that this aristocrat with his refined tastes despised Richardson's plebeian coarseness, he could not entirely escape his influence. In his first novel, *Joseph Andrews* (1742)—the story of a chaste brother of Richardson's not-so-chaste Pamela Andrews—he began with a lighthearted parody of *Pamela*, but was increasingly carried away by the spirit of ridicule into crude burlesque. His Hogarthian wit undergoes similar exaggeration in his second novel, *Jonathan Wild*. In all of this he could draw on the mock epics of English classicism, and apply the antiquated devices of allegories and mythical figures to the modern middle-class novel, deriving comic effect from the contrast.[21] But in his principal work, *Tom Jones* (1749), he succeeded in incorporating Richardson's moralistic and emotional sentimentalism, and even his melodrama, while tempering, balancing, and making economical the whole by ironic characterization. In his last novel, *Amelia* (1752), such characterization predominates.

Fielding, too, like Richardson and Defoe, was still writing with a didactic intention. "I declare," he puts it in the dedication of *Tom Jones*, "that to recommend goodness and innocence hath been my sincere endeavour in this history. . . . Besides displaying that beauty of virtue which may attract the admiration of mankind, I have attempted to engage a stronger motive to human action in her favour, by convincing men, that their true interest directs them to a pursuit of her."[22] Although he was conscious of the complexity of the psychic life, he works out the contrasts of good and evil almost more acutely than Richardson. Tom Jones's half-brother Blifil is a model scoundrel from start to finish, and Sophia's fate makes the book a sort of *Clarissa* with a happy ending. But in his descriptions of subsidiary characters, whether he casts an amiable or sardonic light upon them, he dis-

[21] "Now the rake Hesperus had called for his breeches, and having well rubbed his drowsy eyes, prepared to dress himself for all night. . . . Now Thetis, the good housewife, began to put on the pot, in order to regale the good man Phoebus after his daily labours were over. In vulgar language, it was in the evening when Joseph attended his lady's orders" (*Joseph Andrews*, Book I, Chap. VIII).

[22] Everyman's Library Edition (London and New York, 1922).

plays the keen discrimination which shows that he has learned from Richardson and probably from Marivaux as well. Even more explicit than in these mentors is Fielding's criticism of the ruling class, his sympathy for the lower orders and for those social outcasts whose lives have been ruined by innocent inhumanity.

The most important and fruitful of the innovations that Fielding introduced into narrative is the combination of satire and sentiment. Fielding was not only the first to employ this combination; he actually made it the theoretical basis of the novel form. In his preface to *Joseph Andrews* he calls the new novel, in contrast to the old mythic, chivalric, and adventure "romances," "a comic epic poem in prose."[23] What is meant by that phrase emerges more clearly as he goes on to define his theory of the ludicrous. True misfortune, he says, and real wickedness cannot be the objects of mockery. It would be monstrous and offensive to humane feeling to attempt to make poverty and wretchedness, or the crimes of Nero, ridiculous. The sole legitimate source of the ludicrous is, to his mind, affectation, whether it derives from vanity or hypocrisy. All comedy springs from the contrast between true and pretended conditions. Serious misfortunes call for compassion, overt evil for repugnance; only pretensions and hypocrisies ought to be subject to satire.

[23] ". . . differing from comedy, as the serious epic from tragedy: its action being more extended and comprehensive; containing a much larger circle of incidents, and introducing a greater variety of characters. It differs from the serious romance in its fable and action, in this; that as in the one these are grave and solemn, so in the other they are light and ridiculous; it differs in its characters by introducing persons of inferior rank, and consequently, of inferior manners, whereas the grave romance sets the highest before us: lastly, in its sentiments and diction; by preserving the ludicrous instead of the sublime."

In practice Fielding did not observe this distinction
in all purity, and thus he somewhat undercuts his theory.
In his novels irony and feeling constantly pass into one
another like iridescent colors, and his most lovable character, Parson Adams, a forerunner of Tristram Shandy's
Uncle Toby, innocently and illogically combines both
irony and feeling. The result is a gentle caricature of the
simple in heart. What we are really laughing at here, and
in a good many of Fielding's other characters, is the contradiction between the well-meaning and altruistic side
of the personality and a robustly selfish world.

In other respects also Fielding expanded the form of
narration. His novels are sown with discussions of moral
psychology and aesthetics. In the prefaces and theoretical commentaries which lead off each section in the novels, he offers his reflections on artistic technique. As we
have seen, Marivaux' Marianne meditated on the difficulty of grasping a character in its entirety. In Fielding
such musings extend to the composition of the work as a
whole. He shows that he is fully aware of the newness
of what he is doing when, for example, he emphasizes
the freedom of his artistic choices, in comparison to
Richardson's naïve circumstantiality. In so doing he inadvertently touches on the modern problem of the dis-
tinctive qualities of time:

> Such histories . . . do, in reality, very much resemble
> a newspaper, which consists of just the same number of
> words, whether there be any news in it or not. They
> may likewise be compared to a stage coach, which per-
> forms constantly the same course, empty as well as full.
> The writer, indeed, seems to think himself obliged to
> keep even pace with time, whose amanuensis he is. . . .
> Now it is our purpose . . . to pursue a contrary method.
> When any extraordinary scene presents itself . . . we
> shall spare no pains nor paper to open it at large to our

reader; but if whole years should pass without producing anything worthy his notice, we shall not be afraid of a chasm in our history; but shall hasten on to matters of consequence, and leave such periods of time totally unobserved. . . . My reader then is not to be surprised, if . . . he shall find some chapters very short, and others altogether as long; some that contain only the time of a single day, and others that comprise years; in a word, if my history sometimes seems to stand still, and sometimes to fly. For all which I shall not look on myself as accountable to any court of critical jurisdiction whatever; for as I am, in reality, the founder of a new province of writing, so I am at liberty to make what laws I please therein.[24]

Along with this assertion that his artistic procedure is fully conscious, Fielding unabashedly lays claim to artistic sovereignty: "And these laws, my readers, whom I consider as my subjects, are bound to believe in and to obey. . . ." A significant turning point has been reached: the artist already regards himself as an autocrat in the domain of his material. It is he who decides what he wants to present and how he will do so. Yet he is still keenly concerned about his readers and anxious to placate them: "I do hereby assure them [the readers] that I shall principally regard their ease and advantage in all such institutions: for I do not, like a *jure divino* tyrant, imagine that they are my slaves, or my commodity. I am, indeed, set over them for their own good only, and was created for their use, not they for mine."[25]

Here we may already catch a glimpse, in the bud, of the modern dilemma of the artist: that the reader's demands, the reader's receptivity, stand opposed to the "laws" of the artist's vision, to his new way of looking at

[24] *Tom Jones*, Book II, Chap. I.
[25] *Ibid.*

reality. Subsequently, as the artistic vision and with it artistic craftsmanship develop greater depth and complexity, less and less heed is paid to the actual reader. The imperative of probing vision, and the need to express the consequences of it, become overwhelming.

The development of narration has recently been considered by several critics in terms of the relationship between the narrator and the reader.[26] In fact, a decisive transformation in this relationship took place in the eighteenth century—or to be more precise, a transformation of both the readership and the narrator, and hence of their interaction with each other. The reasons are social, thematic, and technical in nature, and it is difficult to identify the separate strands. Both the mythic-heroic and the anecdotal types of narration in earlier centuries always had a ready audience; colorful stories and adventures, gossip about heroes and courtiers, entertain everybody. The looser and lighter, the more exciting and racier they are, the more they entertain. There was no need for the author to be specially concerned about the reader, and where on occasion he did directly address the reader, that was a rhetorical flourish. In the eighteenth century, however, such addressing became specific and serious. The reason lay, it seems to me, chiefly in the increasing moral, social, and political seriousness of the narrated material. We have pursued this thematic change from Defoe to Richardson and Fielding, and we have seen how the puritanical surveillance of the psychic life

---

[26] I particularly recommend two highly suggestive papers: Victor Lange, "Erzählformen im Roman des achtzehnten Jahrhunderts," *Anglia, Zeitschrift für englische Philologie* 76 (1958): 129-144; and Wolfgang Kayser, "Wer erzählt den Roman?" *Die neue Rundschau* 68, No. 3 (1957): 444-459 (reprinted in *Jahrbuch 1957 der deutschen Akademie für Sprache und Dichtung* [Heidelberg and Darmstadt, 1958], pp. 21-40).

and the widespread revolt against hypocritical class conventions added moral burdens and psychic depths to narrative, imposing inner coherence upon it—or, in brief, internalizing it. In this process satire served either as an expression of revolt or (like the erotic additives) a vehicle of moralistic intention. Conversely, didactic intention sometimes served, as in the case of Defoe, as a pretext for dwelling upon prohibited subjects.

In any case, moralistic puritan narrative and sociocritical narrative could no longer count on a general and easily satisfied audience. The readership for these works was at once more limited and more complex: the social criticism appealed to the progressive and discontented groups, the moralistic puritanism to certain elements of the middle class. The narrator addressed these readers explicitly in pointing out the ultimate meaning of his tale. The seriousness of the themes, the reflections or instruction stored within the story gave a new intensity to the relationship of narrator and reader. For a new strategy was needed to hold the reader. The loose series of experiences offered by the adventure novel could be followed without effort; the new, inwardly coherent narrative demanded concentrated attention. In order to be constantly tightening the springs of his narrative, the storyteller must remain permanently in the vicinity, permanently on the scene. He intervenes personally in the narrative, testifying to the truth or extreme probability of the events, persuading, arguing, almost conversing with the reader. Thus there develops a direct and intimate relationship of narrator to audience, and the latter more and more becomes a personal, individualized reader.

Once again there is a reciprocal effect, for the character of the narrator is also changed. By his very intimacy with the reader the narrator himself becomes more personal, more subjective. With Fielding this evolution goes so far that in describing the girl Sophia in *Tom Jones* he alludes to his own wife, as though the reader must have known her: "most of all she resembled one whose image can never depart from my breast, and whom, if thou dost remember, thou hast then, my friend, an adequate idea of Sophia."[27] Swift, in his preface to *A Tale of a Tub*, expresses the fear of becoming dated and "with the first shifting of the present scene" no longer being understood. Reaching out to the reader of the future, Swift begs him to put himself into the most immediate and private circumstances in which the story was written; to consider that this work was composed in bed in an attic room, that the author occasionally ("for reasons known only to him") had stimulated his imagination by hunger, and that the whole work was begun, continued, and completed during a period of medical treatment and great want of money. Sterne actually insists that the story must be a dialogue with the reader: "The truest respect which you can pay to the reader's understanding, is to halve this matter amicably, and leave him something to imagine, in his turn, as well as yourself. . . . To keep his imagination as busy as my own."[28]

This urge to establish the most intimate connection with the reader leads, paradoxically, to a new artificial aloofness on the part of the narrator. In order to achieve the fullest immediacy and presentness, the real author of the first-person novel and the epistolary novel interposes a fictional intermediary narrator.[29] Examples are Abbé

---

[27] *Tom Jones*, Book IV, Chap. II.

[28] *Tristram Shandy*, Book II, Chap. XI. Text is quoted from the Everyman's Library Edition (London, 1912).

[29] The secondary, interposed narrator reappears first as a survival from the framework story, such as the *Thousand and One Nights*, the *Decameron*, etc. Later on, in the eighteenth century, this narrator is assigned his own proper part as a highly personal

Prévost's Chevalier Des Grieux, Marivaux' Marianne, Defoe's Crusoe and his several female characters who tell the story in the form of confessions, Richardson's correspondents, Sterne's Tristram Shandy, and so on. From that point on down to our own times, this method of disguising the author has remained in constant use, subject to many variations and complications. It has served as a psychological device as well as an artistic tool. (In *Gulliver's Travels* we can already find a triple hierarchy of narration: Swift; Richard Sympson, the editor who both abridges and comments on Gulliver's notebooks; and Gulliver himself. In *The Sorrows of Werther* this tripartite division is woven even more subtly into the texture of the novel.) In any case, whether the original narrator, the *auctor*, slips into the skin of his secondary narrator or into the psyches of the characters themselves, as in the diary, the memoir, the interior monologue, and the ubiquitous free association; or whether, as Flaubert does, he merges himself into the objective event—in all such cases he vanishes again as an individual. For he has objectified himself. And in the course of time his partner, the specific reader, also disappears. This change flows naturally, it seems to me, from the nature of narrative as a craft conscious of itself. Human conditions and relationships grow increasingly dubious and many-layered; social and intellectual processes interfere more and more forcefully with the individual psyche; and in the effort to capture this complexity the artist becomes more

---

mediator intended to hold the reader, afterwards to put a distance between the original narrator and the subject, thus making the story more convincing by objectifying it. The device serves further, in the special case of Conrad Ferdinand Meyer, to permit the narrator to keep aloof from himself. Finally, in Thomas Mann's *Doktor Faustus*, the technique leads to a splitting of the narrator.

and more concerned with the form in which he wishes to present his material. Occupied as he is with this basic task of grasping artistically an excessively complicated reality, the narrator necessarily loses sight of his reader and the reader's receptivity. He can no longer afford to consider all that. The specific reader and the reader's imagination lag far behind him; generations intervene between the author and the comprehending recipient of the narrative. The artist becomes the complete autocrat.[30] Surely it can scarcely be maintained that Goethe in his *Wahlverwandtschaften* and *Märchen*, let alone *Wilhelm Meisters Wanderjahre*, was still concerned about the "ease and advantage" of his contemporary audience. He was concerned solely with expressing his vision as perfectly as possible. And the same is true for all the probing epic prose of our time, from Joyce, Kafka, Musil, Broch, and Elisabeth Langgässer to the most recent experimental French writers. Broch's *Der Tod des Vergil* (*The Death of Virgil*) certainly contains a highly urgent human message; but while he was working on the novel Broch himself once remarked, when asked about it: "You know, it's really no longer readable."

No doubt all such narration remains human communication, and no doubt the author wants the right audience. But the members of this audience no longer sit face to face with him, where he can instantly address them; they have become imaginary. Early, naïve storytelling proceeded from a rather unsubtle narrator to a ubiqui-

---

[30] Where this happens, the serious work of art basically ceases to be a form of entertainment, as it has always been in the past and continued to be even in those eighteenth-century works intended to be edifying. Art itself, the unconstrained interpretation of life that it develops and presents in symbols, then produces the kind of exaltation formerly reserved solely for religion.

tous and tangible listener. Serious, weightier narrative, which begins in the eighteenth century, involves a personal relationship between a narrator who steps forth in all his subjectivity and a virtually individualized specific listener whom the author holds by the lapel, so to speak. The later modern narrator is an impersonally objectified artistic consciousness caught up in the labor of expression, addressing itself to a no longer specific, an imaginary recipient. In fact, the work requires, demands, and shapes its own ideal recipient. This imaginary recipient is included within the work of narration; he is immanent in the narrative and the narrator.[91]

The new forms of experience and presentation that Fielding began or further developed—the combination

[31] In the essay referred to above (note 26), Victor Lange rightly stresses how vital the new insight into the flexibility of *language* was to the development of the novel in the eighteenth century. He points out that "the patent flexibility of the poet toward his subject (and ultimately toward himself) is of course the consequence of a greater flexibility in seeing and judging. But beyond that it is primarily due to the realization which underlies the modern concept of the novel, and of fiction in general, to wit, recognition of the flexibility of language. . . . To the degree that speech forfeits its absolute reference to things, sensations or concepts; to the degree that the relationship of the speaker to the subject and to other speakers becomes flexible and ambiguous—to that degree the novel becomes possible and meaningful as a form of hypothetical statement about human conduct." Here I object only to the "primarily." Seeing is not only equal in importance to speaking and involved in the closest interaction with speaking; rather, it seems to me the more primary human function. What else is speech if not the expression of things seen and recognized? And only perception of the fullness and complexity of reality gives rise to the uneasy recognition of how unstable and dubious language is, how uncertain its grasp of reality. The earliest evidence for this experience of which I am aware is the passage from *Marianne* quoted above.

of satire and sentiment, the occasional admixture of scholarliness, the sententious and theoretical interpolations, the digressions into background stories and interpolated anecdotes, the practices of a conscious artistic intelligence—all this was carried to an extreme and beyond the extreme twenty years later by Laurence Sterne in his *Tristram Shandy* (1760-1767). This incomparable book, this quintessence of whimsicality, which juggles all the elements of narrative in a lordly and totally self-indulgent manner, is both unique and the perfect model of English eccentricity, of that peculiarly English aptitude for penetrating from somewhere beyond objects, from casualness and externality, from peripheral, hyper-peripheral irony, into the most serious heart of the matter. Its experiments make it the close kin, both in its viewpoint and its literary technique, of some of our most recent novels.

In *Tristram Shandy* all the elements and forms of previous narrative are mingled with one another—in fact, this mingling is itself one of the traditional elements. The various strands of heritage and influence are obvious. Nevertheless, the way these ingredients are handled is entirely personal, and the result wholly new.

Comparison with Rabelais is even more compelling in the case of Sterne than of Swift, and has generally been made—all the more so since Sterne himself frequently referred to Rabelais as his favorite writer. The baroque piling up of phrases and repetitions that occurs now and then in Sterne is like a tribute to his great predecessor, implicit quotations. In addition to the literary influence of Rabelais and of Robert Burton's eclectic and rather static *Anatomy of Melancholy* (1621), traces of the *Moyen de parvenir*, attributed to Beroalde de Verville (1610), can be recognized in *Tristram Shandy*. That work is a parodistic symposium of characters from all ages and all realms of life, rulers and poets, philosophers and jurists, church fathers and harlots, who entertain one another with stories of lechery and gluttony and with learned observations; the book is intellectualized and mannered, and presented under punning headings.

Cervantes, to whom Sterne pays tribute as expressly as he does to Rabelais, comes out in Parson Yorick on his Rosinante, in Uncle Toby and his servant friend, Corporal Trim, who play war in their miniature forts on the bowling green behind the house. Swift, of course, is detectable, not so much his *Gulliver's Travels* as his clever allegorical satires *A Tale of a Tub* and *The Battle of the Books* with their deliberate digressions and their recommendation of intellectual "ragouts" and "olios" spiced with scholarship.[32] From Marivaux, Richardson, and Fielding come the additives of sentiment, psychological characterization, and spiritual meditation which are cooked up into the "ragout." Sterne read everything. He devoured an enormous quantity of reading matter from many periods and countries, enjoyed all he read, and exploited it superbly—as, in general, he enjoyed his life with all its marital, physical, and financial miseries, and even enjoyed literary success.

Rabelais, Swift, and Sterne represent three stages in a line of tradition, three steps of rising consciousness and concentration. At the same time they represent a geometrical progression in irony. In Rabelais the wide vari-

---

[32] ". . . I think the Commonwealth of Learning is chiefly obliged to the great *Modern* Improvement of *Digressions*: The late Refinements in Knowledge, running parallel to those of dyet in our Nation, which among Men of a judicious Taste, are drest up in various Compounds, consisting in *Soups* and *Ollio's*, *Fricassées* and *Ragousts*" (*A Tale of a Tub*, ed. Herbert Davis [Oxford, 1939], Sec. VII, "A Digression in Praise of Digressions").

ety of substances are still tossed together in wild confusion, in whatever disorder this Falstaffian quaffer of life's drafts came upon them.[33] His mockery is a form of jesting, bursting with originality. With Swift, the entire work is directed by a superior consciousness. His somber, earnest satire has hidden depths; it is full of tricks, satire upon himself, satire upon satire. In the preface of *A Tale of a Tub*, for example, he says: "But I forget that I am expatiating on a Subject, wherein I have no concern, having neither a Talent nor an Inclination for Satyr. On the other side, I am so entirely satisfied with the whole present Procedure of human Things, that I have been some years preparing Materials towards *A Panegyrick upon the World*; to which I intended to add a Second Part, entituled, *A Modest Defence of the Proceedings of the Rabble in all Ages*." In Sterne, too, the miscellaneous materials and techniques are employed with full awareness on the author's part. Indeed, so clear is his conception that he pushes the whole thing to playful extremes, applying all given and known elements inversely, turning them against themselves, as it were. The irony is not only perpetual and bottomless; it is also engaged in constant self-intensification. It is forever effervescing and brimming over its limits. In practice, here is the beginning of Romantic irony. The wit is even more concentrated, livelier, more complicated, and more cryptic than in Swift.

Eccentricity of method permeates Sterne's entire book, from the outline down to every detail. The book itself is entitled *The Life and Opinions of Tristram Shandy*. Of the life, the only facts that are presented are

---

[33] The etymology of "Pantagruel" that Rabelais himself gives (in the second chapter of Book II) is the Greek *panta* ("everything") and the Arabic *gruel* ("thirsty").

the begetting and birth (in Book III) of the hero, with a variety of mishaps; and toward the end a short journey. The reader can deduce Tristram's education from his father's pedagogical theories, the "Tristrapaedia," or rather from the disregard of these theories. His married life is suggested by a few allusions to his "dear, dear Jenny"—but even this remains uncertain, for the story of his marriage has been reserved for a chapter never written.[34] Given the pattern and nature of the book, moreover, it does not seem that the novel, no matter how long it might have been spun out beyond the existing nine books, would ever have arrived at a direct account of Tristram's life. His life, then, *is* his opinions, both his own and his family's. It is the inner life of the family, the members, discourses, and destinies of the family, that emerge so well described from the whole. Tristram Shandy himself is, as it were, the empty space defined indirectly, like the eye of a storm, by the atmosphere of his surrounding familial home.

This family is respectably middle-class, or rather, like the Harlowes, a middle-class-minded family of country gentlemen, with all the ceremonial and moralistic trappings of such an English household. But apart from this basic similarity there is a world of difference between the two families. The Shandys are as amiable and receptive to the outside world as the Harlowes are stern and narrow. The Harlowes represent fully the rigid formality of middle-class prosperity. With the Shandys, such prosperity is merely the background. For this family consists, moreover by tradition, of pure "originals," eccentric deviants and anomalous variants from the type. The middle class is merely a foil for these "oddballs." Tristram Shandy chooses to describe the principal mem-

[34] Cf. Book I, Chap. XVIII.

bers of his family, his father and his Uncle Toby, in terms of their eccentricities, of their hobbies and foibles.[35]

The droll and endearing character of Uncle Toby comes through in the course of the account of his obsession with fortification techniques. He is shown reviving the campaigns in which he participated as a captain along with his Corporal Trim, and other campaigns that he has studied historically. This brave soldier, who was wounded at the siege of Namur, now spends his days playing war games. He burns with passion when, with Corporal Trim, he razes fortresses or obstinately defends them. But in his personal life this same person is the gentlest, most forbearing of souls, defenseless against all importunities. So tenderhearted is he that after having been plagued for a long time by a bluebottle fly and finally capturing it, he releases it again with the charming words: "go, poor devil, get thee gone, why should I hurt thee?—This world surely is wide enough to hold both thee and me."[36] In his elaborately staged amorous offensive against the Widow Wadman, who has been beyond conquest since she herself long ago maneuvered the innocent fellow into his courtship—in this priceless intrigue a war game and a love game are closely interwoven.

Toby's brother, Tristram's father, is similarly portrayed by way of the vast number of oddities and contradictions that go to make up his far more complicated character. Thus, right at the beginning, Tristram can determine the precise date of his conception on the basis of his father's quirky worship of order. For Father Shandy is a slave of self-appointed rules. One of these rules was that on the same night, the first Sunday of each

[35] "I will draw my uncle *Toby's* character from his HOBBY-HORSE" (Book I, Chap. XXIII).

[36] Book II, Chap. XII.

month, he would both wind up the big grandfather clock and fulfill his marital duties, "to get them all out of the way at one time, and be no more plagued and pestered with them the rest of the month."[37]

Despite such pedantry in his daily life, however, he is inwardly an extremely ill-ordered person, irrational for all his rational dialectics and delight in argumentation, a skeptical rebel, launching at the drop of a hat into testy eloquence which invariably proves self-defeating. His belligerence subsides as rapidly as it flares up.

> My father was as proud of his eloquence as MARCUS TULLIUS CICERO could be for his life, and . . . with as much reason; it was indeed his strength—and his weakness too. . . . If there were twenty people in company—in less than half an hour he was sure to have everyone of 'em against him. What did not a little contribute to leave him thus without an ally, was, that if there was any post more untenable than the rest, he would be sure to throw himself into it; and to do him justice, when he was once there, he would defend it so gallantly, that 'twould have been a concern, either to a brave man or a good-natured one, to have seen him driven out.[38]

The poor man can hardly satisfy his appetite for speculation and debate within the family circle, since his beloved brother has a totally contrary nature. Toby is taciturn, slow-thinking, and absorbed in his military mancuvers, usually giving vent to his emotions merely by whistling or puffing. Father Shandy's passionate arguments dissolve in the face of Toby's irrelevant replies or his disarming amiability. Discussion is likewise wasted on Mrs. Shandy, for in their conversations in bed, his "lits de justice," she merely parrots her husband's opinions,

---

[37] Book I, Chap. IV.
[38] Book V, Chap. III; Book VIII, Chap. XXXIV.

out of lack of interest. In the wideranging household debates, which crop up constantly on the slightest pretext and in which the two servants (likewise eccentrics), Toby's Corporal Trim and the Schweik-like Obadiah, take part together with gentle Pastor Yorick and Dr. Slop, the gynecological bungler—in these debates only the last is a clumsy but stubborn opponent.

Father Shandy is also irrational in his conviction that given names have a determining effect upon the character and fate of those who bear them, and in his bias for long noses—a bias that has long run in his family. In both these matters fate intervenes to mock him, in connection with the birth of his son. The intended name Trismegistus is accidentally converted at the baptism into Tristram, the worst in Father Shandy's hierarchy of names. And at the delivery the child's nose is crushed as the result of Dr. Slop's clumsiness. What is more, it was Father Shandy who had obstinately insisted on Slop's assisting the midwife. The book is full of such magical, self-generating paradoxes and of such paradoxical magic. Scarcely ever has the malice of objects, the clownish self-complication of things, the chain reaction of minor mistakes, along with their often considerable consequences, been described with such loving accuracy as they are by Sterne. Among the regrettable misfortunes attending Tristram's birth, for example, there is a whole assembly of trivial calamities—the "sport of small accidents." Dr. Slop, leisurely approaching the Shandy home on his pony, suddenly encounters Obadiah galloping wildly around a corner; the servant has been sent to fetch him in a hurry. Startled, the papist doctor crosses himself, drops his whip and, trying to catch it, loses his stirrups. Totally flustered, he slides from the saddle and lands in the mire. Aside from the fussy cleaning which then becomes necessary, it appears that the doctor has also forgotten his instruments. Obadiah must rush off again to bring them. Galloping back at breakneck speed, Obadiah finds the instruments rattling so dreadfully that he is obliged to tie the bag up. He does this so thoroughly that there is no undoing the knots. While impatiently cutting open the bag to get at the forceps, the doctor cuts his finger. There is also the matter of the curtained door, which causes all sorts of other troubles.

These paradoxes of persons and circumstances, comical though they are, are described so extensively and with such emphasis that a picture emerges of the terrible gulf between the human being and what happens to him. The descriptive method is extremely important. This method is not only suitable to the material described— which can be said of every work of art—it also enters thematically into the things described, permeates the material to such a degree that ultimately the two become identical. The narrator Tristram—Sterne's alter ego—is the flesh and blood of what is being narrated; he is at once the product and the creator of the narrative; and the eccentricity of the characters dissolves in the eccentricity of the narrative method.

This eccentricity begins with the complete technical consciousness of the narrator. Sterne as Tristram knows just how a writer should proceed in order to tell a normally organized story coherent in meaning and time. But he would not be the person he is if he did not immediately disdain this "straight line," reject the familiar form, and experimentally make necessities out of virtues. Just as he forms his middle-class family out of its deviations from the norm and describes his characters in terms of their oddities, so also he tells the entire story of the Shandys by means of his digressions. The story takes shape out of the atmospheric conjunction of multifarious digressions, divagations, and parenthetical observations.

Swift had already riddled his allegorical tale of the tub with digressions, but these were fairly regular and bore some close relationship to the story, which was in any case abstract. His were genuine deviations from a continuing story line. In *Tristram Shandy* the various ramblings and insertions are entirely arbitrary and spring from the most casual associations. Moreover, they run rampant; they completely swamp the events in a wide variety of ways. They take the form of speculation, analysis and theory, conversation, even dialogues of the narrator with the readers and with himself, montage and stories within stories, dedications and prefaces which stand in the middle rather than at the beginning.[39] Chronological order, finally, is completely shattered; time is manipulated in a wholly novel way. And nevertheless, each such procedure, wanton as it seems, is purposefully guided by an ironic consciousness.

There is nothing of the moralistic tale in *Tristram Shandy*. Its intention is neither instruction nor satiric reprimand. The social criticism—the ridicule of the upper classes, of clerics and scholars and of dogmas and doctrines—and the presentation of human weaknesses in general come along incidentally, flowing into details. The "moral" that might be extracted from the book remains wholly implicit, in the realm of feeling; at best it may be found in the touching goodness, the "good nature," of the chief characters, which Sterne praises lyrically. Still less is the novel an adventure story; or rather, it is an inverse adventure story, a story of adventures in everyday life, among which are the inner adventures of the imagination, of reflection, of sentiment. Don Quixote's campaign has turned inward. The element occasionally

[39] The "Author's Preface" occurs in the middle of the third book: "All my heroes are off my hands;—'tis the first time I have had a moment to spare."

touched on in Marivaux' *Vie de Marianne* becomes, for
the first time, the dominant element. Everyday life
proves to be an inexhaustible wellspring of observations
and psychological event; sharpened attentiveness reveals
the importance of minor movements and modes of behavior. Here, for example, is the famous description of
Father Shandy's reaction to the news that his child's nose
has been squashed:

> The moment my father got up into his chamber, he
> threw himself prostrate across the bed in the wildest
> disorder imaginable, but at the same time in the most
> lamentable attitude of a man borne down with sorrows,
> that ever the eye of pity dropp'd a tear for.—The palm
> of his right hand, as he fell upon the bed, receiving his
> forehead, and covering the greatest part of both his
> eyes, gently sunk down with his head (his elbow giv-
> ing way backwards) till his nose touch'd the quilt;—
> his left arm hung insensible over the side of the bed, his
> knuckles reclining upon the handle of the chamber-pot,
> which peep'd out beyond the valance—his right leg
> (his left leg being drawn up towards his body) hung
> half over the side of the bed, the edge of it pressing
> upon his shin-bone—He felt it not.[40]

He lies in this position for an hour and a half, and
Uncle Toby sits helplessly beside him. Almost fifty
pages later we are whisked back to this scene when
Uncle Toby makes a lamely inapposite remark about the
misfortune of a grenadier. This has no consoling effect
at all; instead it adds to Father Shandy's despair over the
nose his usual dismay at his brother's irrelevancy, so that
the poor man, who had already begun getting up, sinks
back into his former position. And when at last the time
comes for him to get up from the bed, "he had all the
little preparatory movements to run over again, before

[40] Book III, Chap. XXIX.

he could do it." Here Sterne precisely captures the psychological meaning of that irritation we feel in having to return from fullest despair to an unwished-for state of composure: "Attitudes are nothing . . . 'tis the transition from one attitude to another—like the preparation and resolution of the discord into harmony, which is all in all."[41] And the following psychological insight, prompted by the scene just described (and reminiscent of Marianne's remark about tears) is an instance of the serious depths to which this amusing book penetrates: "Before an affliction is digested—consolation ever comes too soon;—and after it is digested—it comes too late; so that you see, madam, there is but a mark between these two, as fine almost as a hair, for a comforter to take aim at."[42]

Another passage provides one of the earliest descriptions of free association: "the thought floated only in Dr. *Slop's* mind, without sail or ballast to it, as a simple proposition; millions of which . . . are every day swimming quietly in the middle of the thin juice of a man's understanding, without being carried backwards or forwards, till some little gusts of passion or interest drive them to one side."[43] Sterne also holds certain clear theories on the possibility of reaching character through physiognomy; his view is both general and individual, closer to Kassner than to Lavater: "There is . . . a certain mien and motion of the body and all its parts, both in acting and speaking, which argues a man very *well within.* . . . There are a thousand unnoticed openings . . . which let a penetrating eye at once into a man's soul; and I maintain . . . that a man of sense does not lay down his hat in coming into a room—or take it up in going out of it, but something escapes, which discovers him."[44] In fact, such shrewdness of eye marks the entire book.

[41] Book IV, Chap. VI. [42] Book III, Chap. XXIX.
[43] Book III, Chap. IX. [44] Book VI, Chap. V.

Finally, this most articulate of English storytellers repeatedly expresses the modern view of the inadequacy of language, and proves his point by the perpetual misunderstandings within the Shandy family. As he often stated, he had been greatly struck by Locke's study on the imperfection of words. But then again he has his laugh on philosophical definitions in the delightful chapter which precedes the lengthy discussion of noses: "Now before I venture to make use of the word *Nose* a second time—to avoid all confusion in what will be said upon it . . . it may not be amiss to explain my own meaning, and define, with all possible exactness and precision, what I would willingly be understood to mean by the term. . . . I define a nose as follows . . . by the word *Nose*, throughout all this long chapter of noses, and in every other part of my work, where the word *Nose* occurs—I declare, by that word I mean a nose, and nothing more, or less."[45] Or to paraphrase Gertrude Stein's famous remark: a nose is a nose is a nose.

But the most revolutionary and remarkable of Sterne's technical innovations is the way he deals with time. He cleaves it, overturns it, makes sport of it. His game with time, in fact, is the key element in his whole topsy-turvy method of storytelling. It appears to spring from sheer high spirits, but fundamentally the game is a serious one and full of far-reaching anticipations, of dawning conceptions that have only recently emerged into full daylight.

First of all there is the discovery of psychological time. That is implicit in the liberal development of reflections which intrude into the narrative. Reflections are bridges for internalization. Sterne was the first to recognize the

[45] Book III, Chap. XXXI.

significance of psychological time for the structure of the novel; he applied Locke's theory of duration to narrative. In the last analysis I would say that the severing of clock time from psychic time is really the innermost theme of *Tristram Shandy*. ("Oh wonderful, unique, primordial interruption!" Rudolf Kassner calls this severing.) Sterne is completely obsessed with the new insight and reverts to it again and again:

It is two hours, and ten minutes—and no more—cried my father, looking at his watch, since Dr. *Slop* and *Obadiah* arrived—and I know not how it happens, brother *Toby*—but to my imagination it seems almost an age. . . . Yet he knew very well how it happen'd;—and at the instant he spoke it, was pre-determined in his mind to give my uncle *Toby* a clear account of the matter . . . in order to shew my uncle *Toby* by what mechanism and mensurations in the brain it came to pass, that the rapid succession of their ideas, and the eternal scampering of the discourse from one thing to another, since Dr. *Slop* had come into the room, had lengthened out so short a period to so inconceivable an extent. . . . Do you understand the theory of that affair? [asked] my father. Not I, quoth my uncle—But you have some ideas, said my father, of what you talk about?—No more than my horse, replied my uncle *Toby*. Gracious heaven! cried my father, looking upwards, and clasping his two hands together—there is a worth in thy honest ignorance, brother *Toby*—'twere almost a pity to exchange it for a knowledge.—but I'll tell thee.— . . . *For if you will turn your eyes inwards upon your mind . . . and observe attentively, you will perceive . . . that whilst you and I are talking together, and thinking, and smoking our pipes, or whilst we receive successively ideas in our minds, we know that we do exist, and so we estimate the existence, or the con-*

*tinuation of the existence of ourselves ... commensurate
to the succession of any ideas in our minds, the duration
of ourselves ... co-existing with our thinking. ...*[46]

This insight is applied to the narrative itself, where
its potentialities are skillfully made use of. Tristram an-
swers an imaginary critic, who might complain about
the discrepancies between the real time of events and
the time it takes the author to describe them, by remind-
ing him "that the idea of duration, and of its simple
modes, is got merely from the train and succession of
our ideas—and is the true scholastic pendulum,—and by
which, as a scholar, I will be tried in this matter—abjur-
ing and detesting the jurisdiction of all other pendulums
whatever."[47] Having justified himself in these terms, he
abandons himself completely to the spirit of digression.
His father's and uncle's descent of a flight of stairs de-
vours four chapters. And in his consideration of the
consequences of such a procedure he finally makes the
following arithmetical somersault into a past that is constantly being enriched by added elements and is therefore constantly producing new futures. The splitting of
time has resulted in a life lived simultaneously on several
levels:

> I am this month one whole year older than I was this
> time twelve-month; and having got ... almost into the
> middle of my fourth volume—and no farther than to
> my first day's life—'tis demonstrative that I have three
> hundred and sixty-four days more life to write just
> now, than when I first set out; so that instead of advanc-
> ing, as a common writer, in my work with what I have
> been doing at it—on the contrary, I am just thrown so

[46] Book III, Chap. XVIII. The argument almost literally follows Locke's formulation in the *Essay Concerning Human
Understanding*, Book 2, Chap. XIV.
[47] Book II, Chap. VIII.

many volumes back—was every day of my life to be as busy a day as this—And why not?—and the transactions and opinions of it to take up as much description—And for what reason should they be cut short?—as at this rate I should just live 364 times faster than I should write—It must follow . . . that the more I write, the more I shall have to write . . . and, was it not that my OPINIONS will be the death of me, I perceive I shall lead a fine life of it out of this self-same life of mine; or, in other words, shall lead a couple of fine lives together.[48]

But there are still other ways in which Sterne manipulates time. By means of his apparent wanderings he moves his story forward and backward in such a way that the digressions not only enrich the descriptions but are in reality propelling the narrative onward. The characterization of Uncle Toby, for example, is interrupted by an ancient story concerning Aunt Dinah and her affair with a coachman. Nevertheless this story is part of the characterization of Uncle Toby, which thus continues beneath the surface, "so that you are much better acquainted with my uncle *Toby* now than you was before." Tristram comments further: "By this contrivance the machinery of my work is of a species by itself; two contrary motions are introduced into it, and reconciled, which were thought to be at variance with each other. In a word, my work is digressive, and it is progressive too,—and at the same time." Even more illuminating is the following remark: "I have constructed the main work and the adventitious parts of it with such intersections, and have so complicated and involved the digressive and progressive movements, one wheel within another, that the whole machine, in general, has been kept a-going;—and what's more, it shall be kept a-going

[48] Book IV, Chap. XIII.

these forty years, if it pleases the fountain of health to bless me so long with life and good spirits."[49]

This complicated artistic structure has been fashioned in such a way that the work can be continued indefinitely without forfeiting its "equipoise," its artistic equilibrium. It has been conceived as a life work which may be prolonged at will, and consequently has remained open-ended. But although it can go on forever, it is complete within itself at any moment. It is both dynamic and at rest. The interweaving of movements forward and backward, of progression and retrospective digression, produces a sense of temporal coherence beyond the confines of time, a coherence of essences as well as events—which is an extremely modern experience. What is more, the whole thing is marked by conscious experimentation, the author perpetually peering over his own shoulder and openly checking on his procedures. Technical comments run through the entire text; they are literally part and parcel of the narrative. The method of presentation, as I have already said, permeates and sustains what is being presented.

The combination of progression and digression prompts further playing with chronological order, a sly game of hide-and-seek with the reader, who is being at once piqued and hoodwinked. There is a building up of suspense to a certain event; then suddenly comes a digression, which postpones the promised revelation almost indefinitely. For example, there is the ineffable complication in Book IX when we at last arrive at the touching love story, the account of Uncle Toby's courtship of the Widow Wadman, announced so many pages earlier. After protracted preparations we have come to the point at which Uncle Toby and his Corporal Trim, who in a

[49] Book I, Chap. XXII.

parallel plot has his eye on Mrs. Wadman's Miss Bridget,
stand at the widow's door. At this important moment we
come upon two blank pages, signifying the omitted
Chapters XVIII and XIX. In Chapter XX we find ourselves suddenly in the very midst of the conversation
between the bashful lover and the lady, who having certain doubts about his capacity for marriage is trying to
find out just exactly where in his loins he was injured at
the battle of Namur. When she asks him, somewhat
circumspectly, where he was wounded, Toby is only
prompted to send for his map. All we are offered here is
the dialogue, along with a short interior monologue on
Mrs. Wadman's part involving the scruples of decency.
We still do not know quite what it is all about; neither
the place on Toby's body nor the map is explicitly
mentioned.[50] The whole grotesque involution of the situation is merely frustrating to the reader for the moment,
and can be fully appreciated only in retrospect, from the
vantage point of Chapter XXVI. There now begins a
clarifying flashback, which reveals the Widow Wadman's worries and her investigations into Toby's state of
health. Full revelation is postponed by an interpolated
meditation in Chapter XXI, a teasing hesitation in Chapter XXIV,[51] and, further along, an episode from Tristram's journey in France—when his thoughts turn to the
question of his uncle's "amours." Not until we have

[50] "You shall lay your finger upon the place—said my uncle
Toby," meaning the map. "I will not touch it, however, quoth
Mrs. *Wadman* to herself," meaning his private parts.

[51] "Though I have all along been hastening towards this part
of [the story], with so much earnest desire, as well knowing it
to be the choicest morsel of what I had to offer to the world,
yet now that I am got to it, any one is welcome to take my pen,
and to go on with the story for me that will—I see the difficulties of the descriptions I'm going to give—and feel my want of
powers."

reached this point—after Chapter XXIV—is something done about the previously omitted Chapters XVIII and XIX. We find ourselves once more outside the widow's door; Toby and Trim enter; and we emerge finally from the labyrinth into a detailed account of the affair.

Such are the tricks the author continually employs to keep the reader on tenterhooks. The tension is increased by the suggestions of indecency scattered throughout the book. These are scarcely ever quite overt; they are gracefully concealed by a drape or left blank, not out of prudery but out of coquetry, as part of the game of hide-and-seek. The reader is given tempting riddles to solve.

In spite of all this, the narrator of this experimental work could scarcely have been able to keep the awkward, viscous flow going were it not for his constant contact with his readers, which is carried to the extreme degree of intimacy. The entire narrative is a continual conversation with the reader, who according to the nature of the subject at hand is alternately addressed as "sir" or "madam" or "your honors and reverences," "your worships," or "my good people," and is initiated into the secrets of the novel's construction or embroiled in imaginary dialogues. The reader's questions and objections are anticipated—and that too propels the wheels of the story. Indeed, the rule is that everything is turned to a variety of uses, is directed both outwardly and inwardly. Even Tristram's addresses to himself and his monologues exert an effect outwardly by reinforcing the sense of the narrator's continual presence.

Since the entire story is a conversation, it retains the spontaneity and stylistic casualness of conversation. The language of the book is—again, for the first time in the history of the novel—intentionally *sans-gêne*. It moves rapidly and with the utmost agility, free of all conventional sentence forms, disregarding grammar, syntax, orderly punctuation; it jerks along through sudden discontinuities and interjections, which are linked only by slippery transitions, obedient only to the whim of the moment. Yet this haphazardness is controlled by artistic consciousness; in the end everything turns out to be in proper balance.

Finally, in *Tristram Shandy* that combination of satire and sentiment which we have already noted in Fielding has penetrated into the very language. Irony glides directly into a lyrical tone; or rather, the lyrical tone is latent in the irony and occasionally breaks out of it to gain ascendancy. In Sterne there are already anticipations of Heine, and the note sounded by Sterne's great successor, Jean Paul, can be heard even more strongly in passages like the following from the account of Tristram's journey in France, where he happens upon a harvest dance and is enraptured by a girl who works in the vineyards:

> *Viva la joia!* was in her lips—*Viva la joia!* was in her eyes. A transient spark of amity shot across the space betwixt us— . . . Why could I not live, and end my days thus? Just Disposer of our joys and sorrows, cried I, why could not a man sit down in the lap of content here—and dance, and sing, and say his prayers, and go to heaven with this nut-brown maid? Capriciously did she bend her head on one side, and dance up insidious— then 'tis time to dance off, quoth I; so changing only partners and tunes, I danced it away from *Lunel* to *Montpellier.* . . . I danced it along through *Narbonne,* *Carcasson,* and *Castle Naudairy,* till at last I danced myself into *Perdrillo's* pavillion, where pulling out a paper of black lines, that I might go on straight forwards, without digression or parenthesis, in my Uncle *Toby's* amours. . . .[52]

[52] Book VII, Chap. XLIII.

Of course he does nothing of the kind for a long time. Finally, then comes the climax of Uncle Toby's courtship of Mrs. Wadman:

> I see him yonder with his pipe pendulous in his hand, and the ashes falling out of it—looking—and looking—then rubbing his eyes—and looking again, with twice the good-nature that ever *Gallileo* look'd for a spot in the sun.
>
> —In vain! for by all the powers which animate the organ—Widow *Wadman*'s left eye shines this moment as lucid as her right—there is neither mote, or sand, or dust, or chaff, or speck, or particle of opake matter floating in it—There is nothing, my dear paternal uncle! but one lambent delicious fire, furtively shooting out from every part of it, in all directions, into thine.
>
> —If thou lookest, uncle *Toby*, in search of this mote one moment longer—thou art undone.[53]

There would have been no Schoolmaster Wuz[54] without Uncle Toby.

This unique book is an end and a beginning, a harvest and a new sowing. Everything that had hitherto been developed is combined and condensed in it. On the other hand, it opens paths into the future. Sterne's material is still the eighteenth-century world, and his idiosyncrasies are exceedingly British. But the strategy to which his eccentricities lead him extends far into our own era. Only today can we see through his oddities and into the depths of his originality.

With *Tristram Shandy* we have reached the threshold of Romanticism. All Romantic elements are already assembled in this novel and brought into relationship with one another: eccentricity and sentimentality, wit and

[53] Book VIII, Chap. XXIV.
[54] One of Jean Paul's great fictional creations.

lyricism, philosophical speculation and the parody of it, scientific empiricism, adventure yarns and fables from all the ages, the shattering of all convention and unremitting, continually self-overreaching irony; finally, along with the released torrent of materials and complications, the struggles with form and the intricate problems of form. In *Tristram Shandy* the thematic reality is already so charged with the patterns, structures, and techniques of consciousness that the creatively working consciousness finds itself face to face with its own image. This complex world, which already includes the phenomena of cognition and imagination—this already half-internalized world—becomes the raw material which is handed on to Romanticism as its reality.

INDEX

Index

ERICH KAHLER, historian, philosopher, and above all humanist, was born in Prague in 1885. He studied in Berlin, Munich, Heidelberg, and in Vienna, where he received his degree. In 1938, he arrived in America, taking up permanent residence in Princeton, where his close friend Thomas Mann was then living in exile. Over the years he taught and lectured widely both here and abroad: at the New School for Social Research, Black Mountain College, Cornell University, Ohio State University as Mershon Professor, Victoria University (Manchester, England) as Lord Simon Fellow, and Princeton University (where he was awarded an honorary doctorate in 1969), among other institutions. He was a member of the Committee to Frame a World Constitution (1945-1948), a Bollingen Foundation Fellow (1947-1950), a member of the Institute for Advanced Study at Princeton (1949), and a member of the Deutsche Akademie für Sprache und Dichtung, Darmstadt. He died at Princeton in 1970.

WORKS IN ENGLISH

Man the Measure; A New Approach to History (1943)
The Tower and the Abyss; An Inquiry into the Transformation of Man (1957)
The Meaning of History (1964)
The Jews among the Nations (1967)
Out of the Labyrinth; Essays in Clarification (1967)
The Disintegration of Form in the Arts (1968)
The Orbit of Thomas Mann (1969)
The Uniqueness of Germany (forthcoming)